Lizard Island

LIZARD ISLAND
A Reconstruction of the Life of Mrs Watson

Jillian Robertson

Hutchinson of Australia

HUTCHINSON GROUP (Australia) Pty Ltd
30-32 Cremorne Street, Richmond, Victoria, 3121

Melbourne Sydney London
Auckland Johannesburg
and agencies throughout the world

First published 1981
© Jillian Robertson 1981
Designed by Andrena Millen

National Library of Australia
Cataloguing in Publication Data:
Robertson, Jillian.
Lizard Island.
ISBN 0 09 137140 6
1. Watson, Mary Beatrice, 1860—1881. 2. Pioneers —
Queensland — Cooktown district — Biographies. I. Title.
994'.3[8]

Contents

On Saturday, the 11th, early... Mr Banks and Captain Cook went to visit the largest of the three islands, and having gained the summit of the highest hill, beheld a reef of rocks, on which the sea broke heavily, but the hazy weather prevented a perfect view; they lodged under a bush during the night... They found it to be about eight leagues in circumference. There are some sandy bays and low land on the north-west side, which is covered with long grass and trees of the same kind with those on the main; lizards of a very large size also abounded, some of which they took.

They also found fresh water in two places; one running stream close to the sea was rather brackish, the other was a standing pool, perfectly sweet. They were surprised to see, from the remains of some huts which they found, that notwithstanding the great distance of this island from the mainland, it was sometimes visited by the Indians.

On their return to the ship, the captain named this place Lizard Island, on account of their having seen no other animals but lizards. When returning, they landed on a low sandy island, upon which were birds of various kinds. They took a nest of young eagles, and therefore called the place Eagle Island...

Acknowledgements

This story, preserved in diaries, letters, official documents, furniture and cobwebs, was unravelled with the help of the following people in Queensland: the former Oxley Librarian, Miss Marjorie Walker, who allowed me to copy Mrs Watson's diary of 1881 and other papers; the curator of the museum at Cooktown, Mr Norman Innes-Will; Mrs Watson's grandniece, Mrs M. Butler; the staff of the Townsville City Library; Helen Mays at the University Library, Townsville; Peter Ogilvy of the National Parks & Wildlife Trust which now controls Lizard Island; Alan McInnes of Cairns; Sergeant Ray Marchant who took me to meet the Aborigines near Bloomingdale Mission so I could hear their ancestors' version of the Watson story; Jill Morrissey; my Great Aunt who wrote letters about her pioneering days in North Queensland; Mr P.D. Wilson of the Archives Department, Brisbane. And also Hector Holthouse whose book *River of Gold* has been particularly useful, as have been the many books and papers put out by the staff of the History Department of the James Cook University, Townsville.

And in New South Wales: Mrs Bertha Oliver, the only living niece of Mrs Watson.

And in England: the Rev. and Mrs Peter Denny at St Newlyn East, Cornwall; the Public Records Office, Kew; Mr Putnam of the Agent-General's Office for Queensland in London; the County Records Office, Truro, Cornwall; the British Museum, London; the London Library; Elizabeth Bancroft and Betty Suchard; Arthur Davidson; Wefe Deliss; Angela Broome and Mr H.L. Douch of the Royal Institution of Cornwall, Truro; Peter Severn and Mrs Sybil Oxnam of Newlyn East; Charles Woolf of Newquay; Viv Scott; my

7

son, James Page, who was so cheerful during the long journeys to research this book; Joan Cambridge, the graphologist, who at the suggestion of Professor Eysenck analysed Mrs Watson's writing; and Brian Edwards who helped with the illustrations.

Also I would like to extend my gratitude to the Australia Literature Board who gave me both a Fellowship and encouragement which helped make this book a reality.

Preface

Twenty years ago when I first stood on top of Castle Hill, Townsville, with my brother-in-law, John Morrissey, he pointed out the islands, the coral reefs in the horizonless Coral Sea below us, as he told of his old flying doctor days up north. Beyond was Fantome Island, the black leper colony run by nuns. The next week, travelling by launch to Palm Island, then a community for Aborigines, I finally arrived in an open boat at Fantome Island lagoon. That was the start of one of the many long stays on that coral cay with Mother St Elvy and Father Maurice Malone, and the start of learning about both the Great Barrier Reef and the haunting story of Mrs Watson.

To my grandfather, Joseph Fisher, a migrant who was a neighbour of Mrs Watson's mother in Gill Street Charters Towers, Queensland. He died on the goldfields at the turn of the century, aged twenty-nine.

The Fig Tree

The worn tombstones, stacked like playing cards against the granite walls of the church in Newlyn East, have left a space where soft green grass grows. There to find what I could about Mrs Watson, I learned that the bones of her ancestors would be joined by only one more descendant. After near three centuries the Oxnam family of gentlemen and yeomen from which she was descended was almost extinct, apart from one surviving man, Eric Oxnam aged sixty-six and arthritic. All that remained as a memorial of that once prolific family was the old school house still called after its founder, John Oxnam, now used for youth club meetings, and the family crest in the church — an oxen and a sheaf of corn.

The vicar had held the living in Newlyn East for twenty-one years without knowing that Queensland's heroine, Mrs Watson, born Mary Phillips Oxnam, had emigrated from his village. The day before my unannounced arrival he had received a request from a bishop in Canberra, Australia, to trace his Oxnam lineage. Was he, the bishop asked, related to Mrs Watson? The vicar had consulted the parish registers for Oxnam baptisms, marriages and burials but he could discover no direct connection. Other coincidences followed: I had set out for Newlyn on the 101st anniversary of the Saturday on which Mrs Watson had departed for Australia; it was also the Feast day of St Newlyna, the patron saint of the village. Furthermore, on the Sunday I arrived the sermon dealt with loneliness on desert islands, thirst, tropical heat, self-reliance and fearlessness. Inspiration, the vicar said, had come from a radio programme. He was unaware that Mrs Watson was famous for adventures on a remote island near the Great Barrier Reef, or that her courage symbolized the struggle of colonists in Queensland last century and had won her a place in a glass case beside Captain Cook and Matthew Flinders in the museum in Brisbane — as well as a marble memorial in Cooktown.

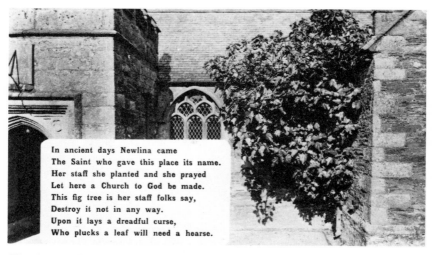

In ancient days Newlina came
The Saint who gave this place its name.
Her staff she planted and she prayed
Let here a Church to God be made.
This fig tree is her staff folks say,
Destroy it not in any way.
Upon it lays a dreadful curse,
Who plucks a leaf will need a hearse.

The fig tree St Newlyn East Church (Ronald Doyle)

I walked around the grey, quiet village and tried to imagine life in the middle of last century when the mines and the fish began to fail. Although holiday-making has now become an industry in Cornwall and the region is dotted with signs for Cream Teas and resort beaches, Newlyn East — just four miles from Newquay and the North Cornish coast and described as 'quaint' — has escaped tourism; few sightseers pass through or stay.

If Mrs Watson and other Oxnams returned now they would find their village of brown stony cottages and houses little different to look at, although the tin, silver and lead mines are empty, no longer worked. Cars replace oxen and horses; instead of three blacksmiths a garage keeps the wheels of the town turning without the smell of burnt hooves, horse sweat and dung. The shoemaker's shop and the tailors have gone, so have candles and oil lamps. Families no longer bother about land for cow, goose or hen. Cheese and eggs come on a van. Apart from these modifications, there is little change; the sense of bygone days in Newlyn can still be felt.

I imagined Mary Oxnam in the 1870s striding up Butt's Hill to church in that plaid dress she wore so often, with a brown belt tight to emphasize her small waist, her dark hair pulled back into a bun. Hitching up her long skirt with her left hand so she could keep up with her two sisters, Nellie and Carrie, calling out, 'One more hill and we'll be on the sea!' She looked determined, proud, almost stubborn. Despite plain features, when she spoke her face took on such animation that she was almost beautiful — some people said 'quite attractive' — and when she smiled the mouth that was too small with uneven teeth, the slightly freckled nose, and the eyes set too far apart, were unnoticed.

12

The church in Newlyn, so important in Mary Oxnam's life, is also unaltered. Fortress-like and holy, for over 800 years it has remained constant, the nucleus of the parish. Before the Methodists built two chapels, St Newlyna's church was a symbol of unity all around. Here every birth, every marriage, every burial was recorded; here the soil was a composite of past inhabitants. The adjacent vicarage was the largest house in the village; it was the vicar who appointed a local farmer every year to act as honorary parish constable. The vicarage is below the place of worship on the highest hill, so just the church with its spreading fig tree is visible for miles around. A climb up the ancient battlemented tower of granite gives a view of meadows, meandering lanes and gigantic hedges stretching to those dark Atlantic waters that touch no land until they reach America. The church was dedicated on 26 September 1259, but there had previously been a Benedictine monastery on the same site. Four entrances, like gateways in a medieval hill fort, lead to the churchyard which stands on an island in the middle of the village. A road encircles it like a moat, cutting it off from the Cromlechs and other pre-Christian and pre-Celtic relics which have marked the land since the Iron Age.

Frequently in her memory, Mrs Watson had said, were bluebells that grew profusely on the hill, and the church itself. The present incumbent, the Reverend Peter Denny, was helpful, producing old records and maps. As his wife, a gentle grandmother, sometimes takes paying guests for short holidays, I stayed at the vicarage, and benefitted from the vicar's clear sense of the past.

On the first night, from the blue bedroom above the kitchen, I saw dark sky intermittently pierced by blades of light: the beams must have emanated from a lighthouse or a passing ship. Far out at sea, mariners watch for the silhouette of the weather-beaten church as a landmark to steer by. The still moments that night were few; gusts from a westerly gale blew in from the Atlantic, hitting our holy hill. Winds in Newlyn are so strong that mists seldom settle; trees are stunted and slanted; brimmed hats are seldom worn. Hedges, ancient and thick, have been grown tall in an attempt to shelter men and animals from the ferocious weather. They give, more than buildings almost, the feeling of permanence, of man's unending struggle with the elements which on this coast hold such sway.

In a way unrelated to the bluster of the winds, I felt the presence of a strange and baleful spirit in this temporary sanctuary, this pretty bedroom. The village was outwardly friendly and ordinary enough, but there was an uncanny sensation, something beyond silence when the wind stopped; quieter than quiet. I had a sense of urgency; despite charming hosts and pleasant surroundings I longed to escape from forebodings that assailed me.

The next day I met Eric Oxnam; he was puzzled by my questioning. No, he had never heard his family mention this Mary Oxnam

13

St Newlyn East Church (Charles Woolf)

who had gone out to Australia and become famous as Mrs Watson; he did, though, talk of his forefathers, their lost mines, their lost money. Despite crippling arthritis, while we talked Eric weeded the garden of his squat terrace house near Newlyn's only remaining pub, The Pheasant. I asked about the church, opposite his house, recurrent in Mrs Watson's memories. He looked up and pointed in the direction of the fig tree.

Through enormous blocks of moorland granite its thick trunk disappears into the medieval south wall instead of earth. The church floor has never been lifted so the home of its old roots and trunk remain an enigma. During the drought of 1976 this fig tree flourished while much vegetation withered; the roots, it was decided, must reach an ancient well. Eric Oxnam, however, was dismissive about its supposed ominous powers.

This tree, centuries old, is described in a leaflet written by the vicar, sold in the nave: '...St Newlyna was a British princess who came from Ireland and landing at Holywell Bay walked to the place where this church now stands. Striking her staff in the ground she said, "Let a Church be built", and from her staff there sprang the famous fig tree... No one knows how old the fig tree is, but there is supposed to be a curse on anyone who harms it, that they will die within the year...'

A belief, generally respected locally, is that a curse protects the tree from being cut down or uprooted, and from the depredations of anybody who — as a verse on a collection box near the tree warns — might 'pluck a leaf'. Fig leaves are often associated with morals and prudery. In the Garden of Eden, figs bore luxuriant foliage; after Adam and Eve had eaten the apple which made them aware of their nakedness, they 'sewed fig leaves together and made themselves aprons'. In Paradise fig leaves were evidence of man's nascent sense of shame. The phenomenon of St Newlyna's fig tree, however, would seem to indicate unseen forces rather than to symbolize modesty.

Fears of St Newlyna's tree may well be warranted; deaths associated with its spell have reinforced belief in its powers. One December morning in 1975, when foliage was breaking window panes and blocking gutters, the church warden took shears to the fig tree. That night, the light of a full moon allowed him to work with his tractor. His safety canopy failed when the vehicle crashed into a disused granite quarry and he somersaulted to his death.

Other instances relating to the tree are spoken of. Even the clergy is not exempt from the bane of the tree. On the first day of the General Strike in 1926 the vicar of St Newlyna directed the sexton to cut the tree back before setting out for the station. The vicar died on the platform from heart failure. Even so, the fig tree and its history failed to impress an Australian who arrived a few years later to visit relatives. He picked a handful of leaves and was buried at sea on his return voyage.

The curse sometimes takes longer to annihilate its prey. The late Archdeacon of Cornwall did not believe in the tree's protective curse. 'On a visit in 1964 he tore off a few leaves saying, "I don't subscribe to these old superstitious",' the vicar's wife recounted. 'He tried to pass a leaf to me! In a few days he had a heart attack; fifteen months later he was dead.'

In 1978 spring came late, in early May no foliage had opened on the fig tree. Eric Oxnam expressed scepticism, 'It has no power', he said. 'None at all. It's all nonsense. The deaths are pure coincidence.' I knew he might be right, but I was still relieved that no leaf could fall in my path at that season to bring misfortune.

I do not know whether Eric Oxnam had touched the tree but doom followed his scathing words. A week after my return to London I telephoned the vicar's wife. 'We have sad news', she said. 'Eric Oxnam was found dead near the coast.' He did not believe in the power of the tree, but something defeated him. Perhaps it defeated Mrs Watson also.

15

Part One

Chapter One

Time,
Place & Ancestry

Thomas Oxnam, Mary's father, believed that God had been man in Palestine. He regularly took the sacrament although bursting with modern intolerances of 'the superstition that abounds in Cornwall'. Some villagers were sure; not even puffed-up Tom could have said, as rumour had it, 'Christ's birth was not on Christmas Day. December's the rainy season in Palestine; there'd be no travelling around then. Christmas is really the old festival of the shortest day; it's a feast to break up dark cold winter. From then onwards days are longer.' Could he have said that? He was supposed to have added that wise monks had fitted Christ's birth in with existing celebrations of the birth and death cycle of nature.

Another issue which Thomas railed against was the timing of baptism. 'Why babies?' he had blasphemed. 'Adult baptism used to be the case.' Eleven years earlier the Privy Council in London had ruled that Baptismal Regeneration — cleansing from original sin — was no part of the doctrine of the Church of England. Conversion to Christianity was itself a symbol of spiritual change. In villages like Newlyn, though, baptism remained to many intents and purposes a rite of purification. A child was carried to the Church through rain, snow, sleet or wind, for if a christening was deferred and a babe died unbaptized its ghost was condemned to wail through limbo, lost with nowhere to go.

Fifteen months had passed, the Oxnam child had not seen the inside of a church. Was this a wild ambition to break all baptismal records? 'Typical of Tom, typical of 'im', villagers murmured. For Thomas Oxnam, twenty-three years old, was a gentleman with boisterous charm and energy, withal a pleasant manner. He sometimes, if unwittingly, alienated both men he warmed to and men to whom he was indifferent. Comment abounded, good and bad. 'Fancy his mother dyin' of the ague when the poor mite was only two', sums up the sentiment brought forward in his defence. 'Drug up like an orphan, he was, and Nanny Roberts never taught 'im to shut 'is mouth. T'would 'ave been better if his father had let 'im go ahead and be an apprentice to a doctor like he wanted to be.' There were other reactions, however.

Not so much tall as powerful, Thomas Oxnam had a strong face, a fresh, clear skin often glowing after riding. With the outer corners of his eyes turning slightly upwards below a broad forehead and with profuse dark curly hair and thick lips he had a foreign look — the stamp of a Mediterranean sailor, shipwrecked on the Cornish coast centuries earlier. An air of superiority marked him; mastery of horses of any description set him apart. He could ride them barebacked faster than any man in the district.

Thomas called his twenty-one-year-old wife 'Martha', pronouncing it rather like 'mother'. He never used her real name, Mary; he had a nickname for everyone. Martha, frail and mousy, was the sort of wife who, if she had only one slice of cake, would present it to her husband. Her devotion and subservience were such that her sentences were copiously larded with, 'Well, Thomas says so', or 'My husband said that'. She dressed neatly but plainly; after seeing her it would have been a task for anyone to recall what she had worn. Even in that era in Newlyn when woe-be-tide the girl whose saucy hat or finery appeared too smart or too fast, Martha's attire was drab. Nor did she 'lace tight', making her figure resemble an hourglass. Despite her appearance it was said that modesty did not rank prominently among her virtues.

Thomas finally agreed to have his daughter baptized. An event such as the Oxnam christening was relished — Sundays in Newlyn could be tedious. Services were long, the sermons repetitive and dull, the liturgy read in monotone. The day, governed by 'Thou shalt not...' made it taboo to entertain, dance, run about or burden servants with work. Weekday newspapers and novels were set aside for bibles or religious books. It was a day to show off a new dress, a time for leisurely gossip. A girl, in between church services and the bible, could catch the attention of a young man she fancied, for Sundays were the only day — apart from Christmas and Easter — when all parishioners came to the village.

Squires and yeomen, accustomed to the timidity of the poor, expected miners, tinners, labourers and cottagers — who still did not have a vote — to know 'their station in life' and to be in their places on church benches at the rear when employers arrived. Scrubbed and groomed, with waistcoat, watch-chain and silver-topped cane, squires lounged in square box-pews in the front of the church, superior both to workers and women. A wife or daughter

St Newlyn East Church (Ronald Doyle)

knelt upon a hassock, but a gentleman bowed only his head during prayer.

The font was at the back of the church so the humble view of proceedings was the better one at that long-awaited christening in May 1861. The object of the ritual, the Oxnam child, to be named Mary, looked rich and much cared for beside the workers in their darned

The font at St Newlyn East Church (Woolf-Greenham)

and patched Sunday best. She was wearing a white dress in fine muslin, tight-sleeved and embroidered in white around the collar. Her gloves, stockings and leather shoes were white. Her age of fifteen months meant she was too large for the Oxnam family christening robe so it was draped over her head of brown tight curls, making her resemble a miniature bride. Upon seeing her someone in the congregation whispered, 'Fancy a child *walking* to her own christening'. An amazed buzz went round the church, followed by pursing up of lips and hurried whisperings. 'Isn't it a disgrace, it won't bode well for the poor girl.' Mary clutched her father's hand, gazing up at this wonderful man with silk tie, tailored coat, gold cravat pin and fragrant flower in his buttonhole. The vicar frowned, looked anxiously around and then stared at the child with the appealing dimples. The mother and two godmothers were ill at ease.

The new inheritor of the Kingdom of Heaven struggled to be on her best behaviour but the chilly air made her baulk at being sprinkled with water. 'Shush, Minnie, be Papa's good girl', chided Thomas, using her nickname.

The enormous Norman font dates from 1180, a time when infants were totally immersed at baptism. Marble pillars rise into the happy faces of winged cherubs which support the heavy bowl decorated by four bemused cats — witches' familiars signified the evil and sin that baptism would, God willing, wash away. Although near the porch this font had earlier stood by the north door so that departing evil ones might conveniently exit to the realms of Satan which, it was thought, lay in a northerly direction. In May 1861, some villagers said that the font should be returned to the north door for christening Thomas Oxnam's girl. Neither Church nor Chapel would forget that fifteen months had elapsed from the child's birth to her cleansing from original sin — initiation into membership of God's Church. 'Why in heaven did 'ee wait so long? I do truly 'ope...' After all, unbaptized infants were liable to be taken by the fairies who carried off children; King Arthur was a 'changeling out of fairyland'. Even today fairies are occasionally seen, for they came back after being banished in Chaucer's day. Adults, too, when engaged in certain unlawful deeds, might, even though baptized, disappear to fairyland.

At last the Oxnam ceremony began. 'Dearly beloved, for as much as all men are conceived and born in si-in...' Thomas Oxnam was sure that it wasn't imagination that the vicar — dark gowned and pompous — mouthed 'sin' with two syllables so as to admonish him for his carnal crime against God. Other stresses in the service were pointed. Martha cowered and tried to repress a blush to conceal shame; everyone in church knew that she had given birth on 17 January 1860, at Fiddlers' Green, down Station Road. She had not been married. Thomas had admitted paternity; he could hardly have done otherwise as Martha had been courted by no other man.

Some villagers declared that conception had occured on the Feast Day of Saint Newlyna, the last Saturday in April. Others insisted, 'No, it was May Day. Saw 'em in Oxnam's haystack...' 'No, no that wasn't them, that was...' That May Day in 1859 had ended happily, wildly. In Cornwall the first day of May was inaugurated with much uproar and in Newlyn it ranked second only to Christmas and midsummer's day. After midnight on 1 May a loud blast of tin trumpets, fiddles and drums proclaimed the advent of spring. Dancing — four-handed reels, six-handed reels and eight-handed reels — followed in barns, including the Oxnam barn at Nanhellon. Much mead, sloe and elderberry wine was drunk before merry-makers set about gathering the May. Young gentlemen, including Thomas Oxnam, joined in the drinking, feasting and dancing.

Months passed. Thomas was absent a lot, travelling. Just before the harvest it began to be noticed generally that the Phillips girl was 'expectin' and 'im not to be seen near her'. Nor was he around for the actual birth. He did, however, enter his name as father on the birth certificate, although Martha was left with the ignominious role of spinster with a babe at breast. Was Mr Phillips going to throw his daughter out of the house for being 'that sort of girl'? Would the birth bring down the blessings of St Newlyna or her wrath?

Despite tears, entreaties, talkings-to, Thomas was scandalously slow to enter the state of matrimony. Farmers and miners might delay marrying until a girl of their choice was pregnant — a courtship might be a trial of fertility. But by custom weddings took place *before* a birth so that a child might have the father's name. When Thomas Oxnam finally agreed to marry, when the illegitimate Mary was eight weeks old, he went out of his way to do it as quietly as possible. He rode eight miles into Truro to obtain a special licence from the Diocesan Registrar which obviated banns being displayed and read in the local church. Everyone knew, though, that the marriage was being performed. Some Newlyn villagers even went to their pews and benches to hear Tom Oxnam utter '...with my body I thee worship...' Others waited outside to watch the couple leave the ceremony. 'Did she take the baby to the altar? Where was it?' the worst sort sneered.

So Mary, our heroine, the future Mrs Watson, though besmirched by remarks like, 'Her father, y'know, wasn't married to her mother when she was born', was descended from two well-known families of the parish, the Oxnams and the Phillips. The Oxnams had been in West country areas since memory began and came to Newlyn in the late eighteenth century. Soon they owned land and mines and had made a mark in the community by establishing the first local primary school. Although Royalists like their neighbours — near the north door of the Church hangs a carved coat-of-arms given by Charles II in gratitude to loyal subjects — the Oxnams never showed the deep attachment to the area felt by fellow villagers. No newcomer who settles in a Cornish district can ever truly become part of it; he can never know the safety of being at home from font to grave, to feel rooted, to be nourished by vegetables grown in a great-grandfather's garden, to walk everyday past the graves of ancestors, to be an integral part of an old and cohesive community. The Oxnams profited from the earth of Newlyn, but then scattered.

On her mother's side, Mary was related to an old family, the Phillips. Forebears of these respected tradesmen were near and around Newlyn before the Civil War, before the Domesday Book,

Coat-of-arms given by Charles II (Woolf-Greenham)

25

before the Norman Conquest. Their long line even preceded cons-
truction of the church in the eleventh century.

The Oxnams, though, grander than the Phillips, had 'arrived'
sufficiently to mix with the best society in the Truro district. They
were minor gentlefolk, educated, having a little Latin and occupying
a huge box-pew to the front of the church. On the whole various
strata of the close-knit rural community did not meet socially; the
sons of yeomen met and married tradesmen's daughters, the
miners' daughters knew and became wives of farm workers and
labourers. Nevertheless, occasionally, a successful family raised its
status — though to sink was easier and many did if misfortune
struck as it did so often during Mary's lifetime through the closing
of mines.

Chapter Two

Nanhellon

After her wedding Martha and her child, Mary — her only dowry — shared a small rented house with Thomas. Later they moved into the home of Thomas's widowed father, James Oxnam. Nanhellon had come to him on marriage and with slated roof it was a gentleman's residence in miniature, albeit lacking the refinements of a smoking room and butler's pantry behind a green baize door. Like many buildings in Newlyn, Nanhellon was granite and resembled houses that children often draw — three sash windows upstairs, two down, with the front door in the middle and a matching chimney at each gable end. It had four bedrooms and downstairs a cluttered parlour, a large dining room, a kitchen dominated by a huge fireplace with a smoky iron range, a larder and a scullery.

Through net curtains the green of trees, the gay colours of roses contrasted with the dark shadows of the Monkey Puzzle branches. A barn lent against the west side of the house and across the farmyard the stables, pigsty, woodshed, fowlyard and outbuildings for ploughs and carts were always noisy with to-ing and fro-ing. A gate in the fence led to fields drenched by torrential rains and fertilized with seaweed and waste pilchards. These fields yielded wheat, barley, fodder and turnips. Mary often thought of this homely and peaceful setting during the troubles that later overtook her.

Her early visits to Nanhellon revolved around her grandfather, a little wiry man who was continually busy — or fancied himself to be. 'Poor dear man', Mamma would say behind his back. 'He really thinks he works hard; a good many people — his son, too — would envy him his leisure.' A mixture of shrewdness, good-nature and irritability, Grandfather dressed formally and neatly, in a style old-fashioned for the day with voluminous neckerchiefs and many frock coats. He had rents to collect: rents to pay; accounts to keep (every

Nanhellon (Viv Scott)

penny received or spent was scrupulously set down). Sometimes a new mortgage was required on his lands; it was costly keeping up with neighbours whose style ran to tea-drinking, dining with fine wines and port, musical evenings and occasional dances. Thrift had died with his wife.

Through the day Mary followed Grandfather closely. If he worked upstairs, she was by his side. When he went to the stables she was with him. When on a shopping excursion to Truro she accompanied him, imitating his example of ignoring the importunities of beggars — he contributed to the parish poor house at the bottom of Butt's Hill and felt that that was sufficient. On fine summer evenings, taking Mary's hand, he strolled along lanes and footpaths, through bracken and gorse; he told her names of trees and plants. 'Come on, Grandpapa', she would say, 'one more hill and we will be on the sea'.

A bond had grown up between Grandfather Oxnam and Mary, for each was, in a different way, an outcast. Grandfather was old, and continually upset by the family's gradual decline. As wind hissed rain down chimneys, rattled windows and banged doors, sometimes Mary lay awake and heard muffled voices in the room below; conflicts between the two Oxnam men surfaced with the port. Thomas Oxnam stretched the use of their land when mining investments no longer gave a decent income. He began to deal in cattle, buying and selling steers — even cows — at local markets, fattening stock on the thirty-two acres; acting sometimes as a wholesale butcher.

The lower social status resulting from Thomas's trading and marriage disturbed his father, but a description of his reputation in the Royal Cornwall Gazette years later should have made the old man proud:

> ...the honourable way in which he has for many years past carried on the business of a cattle dealer. He has been long known as one of the largest dealers in the county, and has been the means of sending off yearly very large quantities of cattle and sheep, thus contributing to the welfare of the farming interest...

Mary, as the eldest child, soon lost the undivided attention of her mother when other children were born. Although not a daughter who demanded affection, she suffered from lack of it. When she seemed aloof or bossy, it was because she knew no other way to be heard; if she flew into a truculent rage, it was caused by pent-up frustration.

If she pestered her father to desist from the tobacco and gin that she was sure would be ruinous, it was a child's devotion and not 'the little mother' in her that was the cause. Papa, who had never been seen rolling drunk, would smile and gently say, 'My girl, those Methodists have been influencing you again! Don't listen to them.' Amused at Mary's earnestness when she watered down the wine and hid the corkscrew, he declared she had indeed grown old before her years.

Nanhellon, a happy house often full of visiting relatives, now filled up with boisterous children: after Mary eight brothers and two sisters were born, although five died. The parlour was soon too small. Used on festive occasions, and particularly on Sundays when Grandfather read allegories aloud from the bible, the room retained traces of former elegance with uncomfortable chaise-longues, fine but dilapidated furniture and large paintings in tarnished frames. It contrasted with the airy stone-floored kitchen — the smells of drying laundry, hot bread, baking pasties, paraffin lamps, coal and sometimes of Mary's newly-hatched chickens. A rigid domestic regime kept house and occupants clean. At dawn the maid scattered damp tea leaves or wet sand over carpets downstairs to lay the dust before sweeping them; at midnight the lanterns were put on the kitchen table ready for burnt wicks to be trimmed the next day. When Papa had found that Mamma had tucked a dull sixpence under the carpet to test the honesty of a new servant girl he exploded, 'Some ghastly hint picked up from *The Lady*, I suppose; a woman's-magazine-Duchess's behaviour'.

On the whole it was a busy, happy childhood for Mary. As the girls, Mary, Nellie and Carrie, got older they went to small parties where Mary and Nellie sang pretty duets. On Saturdays after a family high tea games of Consequence were 'great fun'. When the children seemed bored Mamma would call out, 'Could you see if there's any eggs?', or, 'Take these hot pasties up to poor old Mrs Hosken in the village'. Or, if a rainbow arched across the sky she would ask them to find the end of it and bring back the fairy's pot of gold. Always there was the challenge of the fig tree growing out of the church wall. 'I dare you, I dare you; double dare...', the children would chant, trying to coax someone to pick a leaf and see if the curse worked. See if they lived. See if they died. Papa, of course, said his children could pick leaves. 'The tree has no power, no power at all', he would tell them, contradicting Mamma's caution. 'Well, you never know. Just don't you touch the leaves. Please', Mamma would whisper afterwards.

Far from the pleasant seasonal diversions of the land — the neatness of wheat sheaves after the September harvest, bonfires for midsummer's day — were the lead and silver mines. They were grim. If

The September harvest

30

Mine shaft, Cornwall (Royal Institution of Cornwall)

an awful goblin were to jump out of the holes it would have been less harrowing than the bedraggled miners, thought Mary. The shafts themselves were a source of nightmares — the atmosphere foul with the stench of cheap tallow candles, sweating men, human excrement and exploding gunpowder.

Within a stone's throw of Nanhellon lay the mouth of the rich East Wheal Rose. It was worked intermittently. At off times the pumps, shafts, sheds and engine houses stood like ruined castles overgrown with shrubs and clusters of blackthorn, weeds and blue-bells. The Oxnams could not look out of a window without seeing the mine, the cause of great distress in the village. Water made this mine so costly to run. The terrible danger of flooding has been constant in all Cornish mines — the first steam-engines ever manufactured were for pumping. At East Wheal Rose pumps went down a thousand feet and ran continuously, but they could not always keep the water level safe. There had been accidents, deaths. Gunpowder intended to blast the rocks often smouldered in the damp; when men crept carefully forward to check a charge, it could blow up inches from their faces.

The Cornish have a deeply-rooted belief in tokens and warnings:

31

Tea treat at the amphitheatre (Woolf-Greenham)

fatal accidents, as well as good fortune, are presaged by the appearance of a symbolic caution. Some things were augured to be lucky, others unlucky. ''Tis a forewarning...' was a common remark. The Oxnams, though, shrugged off suppositions that the mine — and the land near it — was unhappy ground.

No mining accident was worse than that at East Wheal Rose described by Grandfather Oxnam when Mary was eleven. After tea on a grey afternoon in the middle of summer, Grandfather took an extra pinch of snuff, his fingers nervously brushed his shirt frill. It was a 'special day'; would Mary go for a walk? As they made their way across the fields in front of Nanhellon, he said sadly, 'East Wheal Rose, Mary, was such a great mine. Exactly twenty-five years ago today it was, in 1846, that disaster struck. The rain had been coming down for days; the mine flooded.

'The men saw water boil up around their feet — thirty ladders to scramble up hand over hand, rung after rung... The terror! It was a thousand foot to safety and the men ahead of you slow and the ones behind pressing and pushing and grabbing. While climbing up, some were overtaken by floodwater, and others fell from ladders trying to get to the top. In the panic thirty-seven men were lost.'

Grandfather spoke on and on; they trudged along the thick sodden turf. Patches of bare land lay here and there, poisoned by arsenic from mine waste; bleak slagheaps rose above fields, across which the banks of the River Lappa stretched in a narrow band.

Grandfather continued, 'So East Wheal Rose closed. Everytime they've tried to reopen it, it's failed. Even after Queen Victoria and Prince Albert had descended to inspect a nearby shaft a few months after the horror, the men would never take their chisels down East Wheal Rose. They say it's unhappy ground.'

'Had the men picked leaves from the fig tree?' Mary asked, although she knew what Grandfather would say.

'Nonsense. You must pay no attention to the superstitions in this village, Mary. Remember, it's 1871, not dark medieval days.'

They came to the large amphitheatre, a Roman-like pit used for Tea Treats and well known because of meetings held there by the Wesleyan and Bible Christians. Hollowed from the earth it dipped below them, through thirteen grass tiers to a small circular patch of grass. Grandfather explained. 'It's a memorial, you see, built by Methodists to the miners who died in East Wheal Rose.' Mary shuddered. Though she had heard stories of a disaster she had never known that the mine she saw when she looked out from her bedroom window was the site of the greatest disaster in Cornish mining history. Grandfather said little as they meandered back to Nanhellon, back to East Wheal Rose. The Oxnams could never receive an unpaid bill without glancing at the mine across the road, reminding them of all that silver locked under the ground.

Cornwall's wealth lay not in the soil, but beneath it, in ores and in what the fisherfolk got from stormy shores — pilchards, mackerel and contraband. No Cornishman can ever be more than twenty miles from salt water with its sea-ways to other lands; in Cornwall roads to change and opportunity always beckon. This Celtic land in the south west extremity of England forms a peninsula so narrow between the English and Bristol Channels that the sea dominates. So much gives the appearance of ruggedness. The rocky coast is indented with deep bays jammed between towering headlands and bold cliffs. The surface of the county is mainly coarse moorland, some mountain pasture; the people are well suited to it — they have to be or they take to those sea-ways which lead to new worlds.

The three sisters, Mary, Nellie and Carrie, walked along Halt Road with a bundle full of saffron cakes and two knitted blankets for old Mrs Hosken. The Oxnams, like all land-owners and mine-owners, threw a crust to the poor before Christmas. Mrs Oxnam made her younger children recite the Lord's Prayer and Gentle Jesus and took delight in seeing them give up their toys to poor children who passed the door. Although the winter was harsh, to Mary the cold made everything beautiful; a land of ethereal trees and whispy strands of mist and gold sunshine. Well-being and gladness filled her as they strolled along. At home Mamma and Nanny Roberts had, at last, got around to putting away summer clothes while the green tomato chutney was cooling in the larder. Papa was with the shoot bringing down pheasants. He had not even been cross that morning when the dog had eaten his left shoe. 'Usually she goes for tastier things', he had said dryly.

Mrs Hosken lived in a cottage made of cob — straw bound with glutinous clay. Moisture rose from the floor of beaten earth, seeped through walls and leaked down the thatched roof, making it damp as well as dark within. It was so small that even Mary had to stoop, for fear of hitting her head against a wooden beam. No luxuries such as ceilings or plastered walls added comfort. The bed was sacking stretched on a timber frame; the only furniture was a rocking chair, a bench and two stools. Over the fire of blazing furze hung a large iron pot in which a broth of parsnips and other winter roots brewed. Nellie, convinced that the soups were not for nourishment but to help Mrs Hosken cast magic spells, said, 'She can wish away warts in two weeks, did you know that?'

Old Mrs Hosken, born the year after the French Revolution began, was thought to be wise because she meted out advice to all she met. 'Did I ever tell 'ee?' she asked, tempting Mary to answer, 'Yes, but I wish you hadn't'. Instead she smiled at the toothless and wrinkled old wretch who hobbled over so she could pluck at her arm. Suddenly she looked at Mary and blurted, 'I tell 'ee that not even the devil 'imself would get ta secret frum me...' Then continued her usual stories, '...and then they fairies made a girt ring...'

At last the girls got away. As they ambled home the feeling of effervescence continued for Mary as Carrie and Nellie giggled about Mrs Hosken's silly fairies. But as the three sisters arrived at the top of Halt Road they met two labourer's daughters, fat and untidy. Hair hung lank down the face and ears of one. The eyes of both fastened on Mary, Nellie and Carrie. 'They do be high and mighty now their grandfa' bought a carriage frum a loord.'

'Well I just advise you not to bother yourself in other people's affairs', said Mary crossly.

'You don't never learn us nothin'!' the girl with black hair retorted, adding, 'What a one. Who's her think she is? So hoity toity, ain't us grand!' She looked straight at Mary, who blushed. Her face became expressionless as the hostile girls whispered.

At home Mary asked why sometimes people nudged one another as she passed. 'It's because you're an Oxnam and because those girls are Methodists. I do think it's wrong that the Oxnam School no longer takes Methodees as pupils. It makes such a division in the village; it's not good, not good at all', Mrs Oxnam rambled on evasively.

Mary felt her mother was concealing something. What could it be? It was baffling and disquieting.

The parish of Newlyn East then comprised 1,688 souls, 500 less than twenty years earlier, in its 8,000 acres. Although the number of blacksmiths and tailors had remained constant — Will Cocking, Dick Daw and Will Tippett did the horses and Rob Tippett and Martin Argall dressed the men — the number of beer-houses and inns in the village had dropped from five to two, not counting Thomas Fugler's Temperance Hotel. The Hawkins Arms, the Eagle Tavern, the Feather's Inn, had gone. This drop was caused by social change rather than lack of demand. The teetotal and upright Methodees had purchased inns and put covenants on them stating 'no alcoholic beverages will be served'. Not only did they disapprove of all alcohol, they did not even sweeten their tea; Methodists in Cornwall had renounced sugar in tea at the beginning of the century as a protest against the slave trade, and the habit lingered. This new wave of Puritanism which the brethren spread affected Anglicans also. Chaste indeed the village was; Mary stood as a living cautionary tale — 'the result of Lust'.

Although the mainline railway system from Paddington now reached Truro, ending centuries of insularity and introducing the tripper, most change in Newlyn was initiated by the Methodist sect with its prudery and false shame. The congregation in Newlyn church was dwindling as many parishioners, the independent or insubordinate, when accused of aping their betters, found a more comfortable alternative in the rival centre, the chapel. Chapel was at loggerheads with Church. Bitter opposition to these 'brethren and sisters' of John Wesley was led by the incumbents of the Anglican parish. The dissenters had erected their own place of worship; on Sundays they now ignored the peals of the five bells rung out so admirably from the ancient, pinnacled and battlemented tower. Vigorous were the non-conformist 'grand old hymns', with their ghoulish rhetoric about Jehovah, damnation and the wrath of God. The terrors of hell-fire awaiting sinners were punctuated by loud 'Hallelujahs!' Shouted in chorus they floated across the village, in competition with the more decorous hymns of the Anglicans who were not so interested in the sacrificial blood of Christ. Oxnams, tenant farmer and publican still stood for Church and Tory, Mr Disraeli and the promise of Heaven; mason, wheelwright and blacksmith now stood for Chapel and Liberal, Mr Gladstone and salvation from hell-fire.

The bitter anti-ecumenical feud between the Anglicans and the Dissenters is illustrated by a note of the vicar's in the margin of the Register, 'Baptized by some schismatic'. The school brought out a new rule: 'No Methodists'.

Chapter Three

Schooldays

The starving sparrow pecked at the frosty glass. Mary shivered as she pushed up the snowy sashcord a few inches and put out half an apple.

'Mary, Mary, quick. Someone's coming.'

Mary sped back to her bed, across the dormitory and pulled up the covers. It was so cold that the condensation on the inside of the windows froze into sheets of ice. Keyholes were even stuffed with newspaper to keep out draughts, but the pupils were forbidden to sleep in their underclothes 'like a common farm worker', or to wear a warm flannel petticoat instead of the crisp cold nightdress. The vest under Mary's regulation night attire was showing near the neck. The day before, she and her two school friends, Betty and Anne, had cheated by cleaning their hair with talc instead of washing it because it was so cold. Although Mary was responsible and had a strong sense of duty, there was a gently rebellious side to her that said, 'Why should I?' During the two years that she and her sister Nellie had attended school in Truro she had had many victories — being 'found out' was rare.

The roads were still bad; a gentleman travelling alone found it easier to travel by saddlehorse than be jolted in a cart or carriage. The poor either walked or went by public carrier. So that the girls would not have to make the journey to Truro every day Papa decided that they should board at the school.

It was 6 a.m. and time to get up. They had to be in the schoolroom an hour later. The routine absorbed Mary. Lessons until eight; then came prayers, hymns and porridge. Fifteen minutes in the garden, and back to her desk until twelve. Toast, vegetable broth, meat and cabbage for dinner, and half an hour's free time. Lessons again till two; then a walk up the hill or by the riverside, drifting home to tea and a quarter of an hour's rest 'to save the girls' complexions', back to lessons again till seven. A hot drink at eight; prayers, dormitory, candles out at nine. As a lady had to have elegant hands the girls rubbed their fingers and palms with lanoline before putting on cotton gloves which they were to wear all night.

There was a silence.

'You wanted to talk to me, you said?' ventured Mary slowly. The air was sweet with geraniums and lily odours. Mary came a little way into the room, stood still and waited. She knew what Miss Moore was going to lecture her on: how to speak correctly. She complained if a pupil's language was punctuated with 'those frightful provincialisms that will never be tolerated in polite society'. 'Where *were* you brought up?' she murmured sarcastically to Mary, adding a broad smile.

'One does not expect you, Mary, to use such uncouth pronunciations as "preventative" — it is preventive! Today I went into town, my ear wrung with such barbarisms as qual-aty, terr-uble, cru-alty. Next it will be yalla for yellow!'

Miss Moore's intolerance was also revealed when a girl blew her nose with a handkerchief using both hands instead of just the right thumb and forefinger. 'Effort, girls, do learn to make that extra bit of effort', was a frequent plea. She was even a little exasperated if a girl, out for a walk, deviated from the prescribed route, especially if this detour took in Mr Hamlyn's confectionery shop at the corner of Lemon Street with its forbidden bunnies of pink sugar and delectable aniseed balls.

'The conduct of gentlewomen' was, of course, a favourite topic of Miss Moore, who would talk endlessly on etiquette: a young lady never sat cross-legged, never scratched, never poured the milk into a cup before the tea 'like a charwoman'. 'Don't say "Pardon" say "What?" ' She also taught the correct times for 'At Homes' and for leaving visiting cards. The girls, forbidden to dance together, learned the waltz by pushing chairs — furniture was a suitable substitute for a man.

During deportment, a separate subject, the girls stood for hours with books balanced on their heads and learned how to bend and lower the body when 'curtseying to Her Majesty' — not that any pupil of this Truro school was ever likely to reach Court, let alone the fringes of the Prince of Wales's Racing Set. Many of them, though, made it to the colonies of the Empire — to Ceylon, to 'Inja' and to Africa — and did their Christian British duty with hands in kid gloves while they saved those pampered complexions by sheltering under green umbrellas. They became the cream of colonial society, so the training was not all in vain. Some ex-pupils were even to wear veils, feathers and white satin gowns with long trains and be gracefully presented to the Viceroy in Delhi. Little did Mary realize that 102 years after she left school, a Prince of Wales, Prince Charles, would visit the ruins of her home on Lizard Island

One girl at school had a mother who rented a house in Belgravia for three months in the spring and started the London Season by driving in Hyde Park and leaving a lot of visiting cards. How Mary longed to go to the opening of the Royal Academy and the party given by the Horticultural Society in the much pictured giant conservatory lit by gas lights and crowded with flowering shrubs. How distant from that world was Nanhellon where the chief excitement was the new prize rooster, Henry!

Miss Moore was also a conscientious and painstaking teacher. 'Oh, dear, you didn't do well with parsing this morning', she would murmur sympathetically to Mary, who was sometimes confused by irregular verbs. All pupils wrote a beautiful hand, almost like copperplate print, and were equipped, like many graduates from similar academies for young ladies scattered throughout the British Isles, later to become governesses in upperclass homes; England then had a thousand Jane Eyres. The few dignified careers such as teaching and music open to educated gentlewomen were crowded; it needed exceptional qualities, training and luck to get a position. With neither votes nor jobs women found marriage the only easy

Truro from Kenwyn (Royal Institution of Cornwall)

alternative to either staying at home with parents or paying one's way as a spinster aunt by darning other people's socks, bottling gooseberries and writing caring letters to nephews at boarding school.

Mary yearned to be a teacher. Although she was often irritated by Miss Moore, a strong bond developed between the middle-aged mentor and her pupil. They shared an appreciation for similar books, although Miss Moore cared for Shakespeare more than Mary did.

'Mary, dearest Mary', Miss Moore would chide, 'You must be more patient. How fortunate you are to be educated... The year you were born only one out of every seven British children of a suitable age to be taught went to school.' She would explain again why she insisted on practices such as stitching up the pockets of the younger girls to stop them slouching. 'Etiquette makes social intercourse more agreeable.'

To her, manners and a Christian self-abnegation were paramount. 'Always be kind to your neighbours and civil even to enemies', she would coax. 'Don't be like barbarians and savages who know nothing of the virtues of forgiveness; they regard a man who is not revengeful as wanting in spirit.'

Some of the teachers, though, were not as strict as Miss Moore. Mademoiselle, who gave needlework instruction as well as French,

Boscawen Street, Truro (Royal Institution of Cornwall)

joined in when the girls calculated Miss Moore's age during needlework, a skill which taught the valuable womanly quality of patience. It was compulsory for both pupil and teacher, and enjoyed by neither. 'Le stickwork I dislike, le 'brodee I 'bominate, le stocking-darn is soo soo dull', she would confide.

Mary had grown into a pleasant, if ordinary looking girl with a face and figure inclined to plumpness. She had reddish brown hair and sharp grey eyes but her looks varied according to her mood. At school they said her deportment was excellent. She found comfort in being precise and tidy, especially after the sad loss of her grandfather, which left her for months morose, red-eyed and more reclusive than ever.

During holidays at home Mary would seek out a quiet spot to which she could retire with her book; normally it was the hayloft, a refuge from the bustle and noise at Nanhellon. Up there day after day Mary read and read. *Canterbury Tales* took a great and fascinating hold on her, as did the novels of Sir Walter Scott and Charles Dickens. Only a few years more and she could escape to independence with a career as a schoolteacher; already she was a prefect.

View of Truro

Trestle Viaduct, Truro (Royal Institution of Cornwall)

Oh, the freedom of holidays. The elation of not being at school to be reminded of 'Our Duty' of thrift, hard work, early rising, punctuality and self help.

Mary, with her ambition to teach, was to be the first female Oxnam to take up the family theme in education. She started keeping a log-type diary when she was fifteen, in training for when she would be recording the activity of a schoolroom.

It was Mary's great-grandfather, John Oxnam, who had built and endowed the first school in Newlyn in 1814 to teach the three R's and to expound the doctrine of the Church of England. The deed of gift, kept in the iron chest belonging to the parish, stipulated that the Oxnam Trust would also donate a home for the schoolmaster, a stipend of £5 and a sum not exceeding forty shillings per annum for repairs to both buildings.

Grandfather also kept up the family tradition of concern with

41

learning. He regularly visited the school after the Diocesan Inspector had examined the pupils' for religious knowledge. Grandfather, a trustee, dutifully read the teacher's log book:

Nicolas J. at home to have his boots mended... sent Jim W. home for coming to school dirty... Elaine D. not at school for want of clothes... several absent on account of weather very rainy... Tom has not been at school for several weeks for want of clothes... sent Polly home for her school money... sent Jim home for being dirty... punished Joseph for throwing stones at the window... punished Betty for breaking her slate...

42

Chapter Four

Downhill

The fortunes of the family, on a downward trend for decades, drew closer to crisis at the death of Grandfather Oxnam in 1872 when Mary was twelve. Although the land, freehold and leasehold, was bequeathed to Thomas — all other sons being dead — it contained cash legacies. 'I give my daughter Elizabeth all singular household furniture, goods and chattels plus £50... and I give my grand-daughter, Sally Martin...' Without money, Thomas was forced to take out more mortgages on the already encumbered land for cash to execute the will and to replace the household furniture bequeathed to Elizabeth — the Turkish carpets, the paintings, the beaded footstools, the velvet chairs, the pianoforte. A new rosewood cottage piano was bought from Collard and Collard in London for £80. One item in the will which caused a terrible argument was a glass case of stuffed parrots and a 'cabinet of curiosities'. Mary's father insisted, in the face of vigorous opposition, that the birds were his. It was one of many a fuss, as now there was much tension. In order to survive, Thomas was living off borrowed capital rather than income; he had entered upon an impossible course.

Mary did not understand how Papa could keep solvent; his business of buying and selling was a minute part of the vast English industrial economy, vulnerable to the uncertainties of international trade, with its surpluses and suicidal competition. The domination of Britain — which since the mid-1700s had led the worldwide Industrial Revolution — was now being challenged. The heyday of her 'commercial Empire' was overcast not only by the United States of America but by the new and recently united Germany. Under Bismark the scattered principalities of the Rhine and Central

Europe were joined into a powerful political and economic bloc, unseen since the era of Frederick the Great. Germany had as yet no merchant fleet to compete in establishing far-flung markets, but her massive industrial cartels were menacing the French and British in Europe.

The farmers in Cornwall understood the situation only through the results they saw in their own district. They were being ruined by inflation, by cheap goods being dumped in Britain by the backward parts of the Empire. Also, England had become so thickly peopled that the soil could not maintain her population. More imported food had to come; more manufactured exports and people had to go. The agricultural depression had begun and was to linger for twenty years causing distress and irregularity of employment. In Cornwall life seemed sadder than in the South and the North. In one six-month period alone over 10,000 emigrants left Cornwall for Australia, thousands went to America and elsewhere. They abandoned their cob and thatch cottages to migrate to Australia, America or New Zealand. Prosperity fell with the price of lead, tin and copper. The colonies ruined Cornwall by exporting cheap tin and minerals to the British Isles, but in return offered jobs and homes to the skilled whom they had thrown out of work. A million and a half Britons left their homes forever during the 1870s.

So many miners were unemployed that emigration figures would have been higher had more men been able to afford the fare or dare the distance to Australia, Michigan or Illinois. By 1877 over a quarter of the mines had closed and miners were paid only three-quarters of their former wages. This decline coincided with a drop in the size of the shoals of pilchards. As a result ropemakers, workers in gunpowder factories, boat builders, shopkeepers and many craftsmen were also jobless.

Mary was seventeen when her father was finally defeated by the pawnbroker, the bank, the bailiffs and the mortgagees. English prisons still received debtors although an act had been passed in 1869 'for the Abolition of Imprisonment for Debt...' A man who did not pay his bills still had the threat of being put in a cell if he defaulted on a court order or judgement to pay money owing. In 1876 nearly 5,000 people were committed to local prisons in England and Wales because of unpaid debts, nearly half the number who were locked up a decade earlier. The maximum gaol sentence was now only six weeks; the disgrace, though, was the same, especially for a man like Thomas Oxnam, were he to be committed. He had been brought up to believe that it was proper for a gentleman — through hard work, planning and thrift — to stay out of debt. Debt was only excuseable as a temporary measure to mend one's finances.

It was the mud and the slush of that dreadful winter of 1876-77 and the torrential rains that finished Thomas Oxnam. Just as the rain augured the demise of the Oxnams with the flooding of the

44

mine forty years earlier, it was rain that finished them off altogether. As mud froze that January, Thomas struggled to keep his property solvent but the forces against him were swept in from too many different directions. The Industrial Revolution had reached its competitive peak. Each consecutive day at market was less successful; money and work were scarce outside the large towns. The silver and gold rings were off Mamma's fingers; there was no coal in the Oxnam grates that winter. The coal merchant, like other tradesmen, made no more deliveries. They only came to plead for payment.

Poor Mamma, she battled so hard for her brood. When the coal heap was nothing but a few specks of black dust it had been Mamma who had secretly crept out of bed on the coldest nights to tuck logs into the fading fires. Papa had thought the fires stayed in because damp wood was slow burning. Like the miners and labourers, the Oxnams were reduced to burning peat out of the moors, driftwood gathered on beaches, furze and brushwood. And now that there was only one maid, Mamma wore herself out washing clothes, scrubbing the wood and stone floors, polishing furniture and fire-irons, baking and. boiling. Poor Mamma was so sweet, so helpless and so exhausted by the drudgery of bearing eleven children and burying four of them. Papa had been indifferent about the pain and discomfort of childbirth; Mamma had hoped that as the cows required his help with calf births he would be more sympathetic, know what it was like when she gripped the lefthand column of the four-poster bed. But he always remained distant, was never there.

If a Newlyn farmer said he was 'going to market' it meant he was going to Truro and it was Wednesday. Newlyn had its own fair where livestock and cattle could be sold locally only once a year in November. Thomas Oxnam rode to Truro every market day and traded at a large number of fairs throughout the area. But one day in February it was Wednesday and Thomas Oxnam was at home. He had no cash to buy and nothing to sell; no man would give him credit after his close brush with bankruptcy. Already an advertisement had appeared on the front page of the West Briton & Cornwall Advertiser:

Notice to Debtors and Creditors. All persons having any CLAIMS or DEMANDS against THOMAS OXNAM, of the parish of Newlyn East, in the county of Cornwall, Cattle Dealer, are requested to send particulars of their claims to Messrs Whitford & Sons, Solicitors, St Columb; and all persons INDEBTED to the said Thomas Oxnam are requested to pay their debts to the said Messrs Whitford and Sons.
Dated St Columb, 6th February 1877.

Thomas, who knew the weight of a steer just by looking at it, could no longer deal. Instead he fidgeted at home, waiting for the mail which arrived at Newlyn from Grampound Road at 10.45 a.m. By the time Mr Johnson Rule Symons, the new sub-postmaster, had sorted the letters it was usually late morning. That Wednesday yet another bulky envelope arrived from the solicitor at St Columb containing copies of letters. One dated 28 March read, 'I quite forgot yesterday to ask you about debts due to several clients, Thomas, Glanville...' Another was from William Glanville, 'In answer to your enquiry Mr Thomas Oxnam owes me £33 9s 5d and I do not know how to get the money. I have sent my account to Mr Whitford of St Columb according to the advertisement. He has promised to pay me next Thursday but I have no faith. If you can assist one I shall be very thankful, your obedient servant...'

Even the sale of the freehold land in February had not produced enough cash to settle the mortgages, the outstanding bills and debts, including the £500 lent by John Williams at 4 per cent and the £350 lent by John Andrew. The Oxnam's twenty-one acres, known as Binney's Tenement, had fetched £1,700. It had gone to Christopher Hawkins, the owner of the other big lead mine at Shepherds, near Fiddler's Green. But there was still a deficiency of money. The house had to go. And the furniture. And Mary's piano. And the family. It was the poor house or Australia.

After the land was sold, even though vacant possession was not being granted until Lady Day — 25 March — the children's pet donkey had to go. The notice in the *West Briton* listed much that was precious to the Oxnams:

Mr Tremaine is favoured with instructions to SELL by PUBLIC AUCTION, on FRIDAY the 16th day of February instant, at Nanhellan [*sic*], Newlyn East, the LIVE AND DEAD FARM STOCK, & C., the property of Mr Thomas Oxnam, who quits his farm at Lady-day next, viz:- 2 milch cows, 6 young bullocks, two years old, 2 calves, 2 good labour horses, 1 horse, rising five years old, 15h. 2in., good in saddle or harness, 1 donkey, four years old, exceedingly good, 15 large and slip pigs. IMPLEMENTS ., consist of 1 corn waggon, 2 cart butts, 1 iron cultivator, 1 double plough, 1 single cart horse hoe, set of iron harrows, chain harrow, sheep rack, winnowing machine, seed machine, wheelbarrow, shovels, prongs, pikes, rakes, iron pigs' troughs, sets of fore and hind harness, set of whips, about 140 good five-bar iron hurdles, and numerous other articles.

About six tons of good hay, rick of straw, several tons of mangolds, two acres of swede and pasture turnips, & c. Also a good Whitechapel TRAP and HARNESS and a DOGCART and HARNESS. Refreshments at twelve o'clock, and sale at 1.30 p.m. precisely.

The above will be found a very useful lot, and well worthy the attention of agriculturists.

The furniture will be sold before Lady-day next, of which due notice will be given in future posting bills.

Dated St Columb, 6th February, 1877.

Mary was playing the piano, her constant solace, when Mamma and Papa entered the parlour to bring her the tidings that they were going to migrate to New Zealand.

'But do *I* have to go, Mamma?' she said. She flew at once to her mother. 'New Zealand!'

Papa's determination that the family should stay together was strong. 'But Minnie, dear, we couldn't leave you behind. I'd miss you too much.'

'I have done as you bade me in everything', she replied. 'Could I not take a position in London as governess until I am old enough to live alone and work as a teacher? Oh, Papa!' How could Papa understand the misery, the utter despair, of not going ahead with a position.

'But why New Zealand?'

'Well, it depends on many things where we go. It could be Australia or New Zealand. I'm waiting on letters about positions and land. Queensland is offering a lot of free passages. I have applied to Mr Davis in Truro, the local agent for Queensland, and have requested details of migration regulations for New Zealand.'

Those for South Australia Thomas unfortunately already knew; he did not qualify for South Australia as he was too old. The government there only granted free passages to 'carpenters, bricklayers, masons, plasterers, agricultural and railway labourers, copper, tin and lead miners, single or married, with not more than 3 children... female domestic servants'. Coal miners were ineligible, as were men over forty.

Poor, dear Papa. 'Of course, you are right, Papa', she said. 'I will go with you.'

'I blame myself', he murmured. 'I wish we didn't have to go. I feel as though I have destroyed myself.'

'Do not say that, Papa', said Mary gently, and then with a smile, 'Think what a nice time Mr Micawber had in Australia. Think of Charles Dickens!'

The Oxnam family were just one of the many who followed Mr Micawber to Australia. Their middle-class background made them susceptible to promises that literature made on behalf of this new land; if in a blind alley in Europe, Australia was an escape. Dickens had said so, Trollope had said so — it must be true. To understand the story of an emigrant such as Mary, it is important to grasp the mixture of failure and hope that accompanied their departure. The failure was their lives; the hope was the picture of the colony that Charles Dickens, Anthony Trollope and others whose work they knew so well had put before them.

Continually in a state of impecuniosity, Mr Micawber, the fat and loquacious hero in *David Copperfield*, was always hoping for 'something to turn up'. His final solution was to take his family on a ship to Australia. Dickens portrayed emigration to Australia as an adventure, exciting and promising, not a last resort. In the last chapter of *David Copperfield* reports were received of Mr Micawber in the new land; he had set himself up on a farm in the bush and was 'turning to with a will'. Seizing every opportunity, he had become a land-owning magistrate. This was the primary theme of literature about Australia; anyone prepared to take fortune into their own

Charles Dickens (Dickens House Museum)

hands, to work very hard, would be rewarded for their effort.

No colony ran a more effective propaganda campaign than Charles Dickens. He thought this newly settled continent was a solution to many problems; a land of special opportunity. In his new and very successful weekly magazine, *Household Words*, he published 'A Bundle of Emigrants' Letters', to which he wrote the introduction. The emigrants talked of a land of plenty. The material problems that beset the less well-off in England seemed non-existent in the antipodes; it was 'a fine country and a beautiful climate' where 'provisions of every kind are very cheap'.

Dickens's own sons emigrated to Victoria in the 1860s and made middle-class emigration to Australia more acceptable. Alfred Tennyson Dickens had sailed from England in 1865 with enthusiasm, and eleven pairs of kid gloves. After two years he left Melbourne for Conoble, a station with 40,000 sheep, 100 miles north of Hay in New South Wales, where he worked for a few months. 1868 found him on the move again, to a new position at a sheep station in Corona. That same year his younger brother, Edward (known as Plorn) also migrated from England for Australia. After many new jobs and fresh starts, by the mid-1870s when the Oxnams were migrating, Plorn was station manager of the half-million acre Mt Murchison Station.

Anthony Trollope went further than Dickens. He not only sent his son Fred to farm sheep in Australia, he visited him twice. He wrote enthusiastic articles about the colonies for the *Daily Telegraph* in London and a 1,000-page guide, 'Australia and New Zealand', which quickly sold out. He also wrote two novels, *Harry Heathcote of Gangoil*, based on Fred's life at Mortray Station, and *John Caldigate*, a gold-mining tale. Caldigate, like Dickens's Micawber, left England because of mounting debts.

Alfred Tennyson Dickens (Dickens House Museum)

Chapter Five

Hope of Another Country

Inquisitive persons — not wanting to miss a bargain or a scene — had come streaming down Halt Road since late morning. At 1.30 p.m. the more elegant, or restrained, arrived in horse-drawn vehicles, small buggies and waggons. The crowd was drawn by an advertisement listed for two weeks on the front page of the *Royal Cornwall Gazette*:

NEWLYN EAST
Superior HOUSEHOLD FURNITURE and other Effects,
for Sale

MR TREMAINE is favoured with instructions to SELL by PUBLIC AUCTION, on Friday, the 27th of April inst. at Two o'clock in the Afternoon, at NANHELLAN [*sic*], in the Parish of Newlyn East, the whole of the

MODERN HOUSEHOLD FURNITURE

the property of Mr Thomas Oxnam, who is about to leave his residence; comprising mahogany tudor, four-post, iron and other bedsteads, with furniture; matresses, 4 feather beds, with bolsters, pillows, and other bed linen; mahogany and other chests of drawers; dressing tables, wash-stands, looking-glasses, toilet sets, towel airers; bedside, stair, and other carpeting; stair rods, bedroom chairs.

PARLOUR — Mahogany pillar table, 6 hair-seated chairs, easy chair, mahogany chiffonier, ladies' work tables, large mirror; chimney orna-ments, silver-plated tea service, case of foreign birds, double-burner lamp, tapestry carpet 12 feet by 12, hearth rug, fender and set of fire irons.

LOBBY — Bronze umbrella stand, barometer, pair of Spanish horns; cocoa-nut and wool mats, and passage canvas.

KITCHENS — Mahogany dining table, couch, arm and other chairs, coal scuttle, copper kettle, brass and other candlesticks, pictures, cup-board, deal tables and forms, writing desk, bacon rack, meat safe, meat

51

cooler, stugs, paste board, milk pans, buckets, washing trays, washing machine, boilers, kettles, saucepans, dinner sets, and a useful lot of earthenware, a good double barrel gun, and numerous other articles.

Also, an excellent rosewood cottage PIANOFORTE (by Collard and Collard, London), compass 7 octaves (lately new).

The *AUCTIONEER* in drawing attention to this Sale, begs to observe that the above furniture will be found in good condition, and will be sold without reserve, and as the lots are numerous he solicits an early attendance.

The Sale to commence punctually at Two o'clock in the Afternoon. Dated St Columb, 13th April, 1877.

Mary watched the women invade Nanhellon; women with eyes like anglers anticipating a catch, picking up the dear belongings and putting them down again; loved objects numbered and catalogued, now no longer her's. They groped with delight among things that might soon be their very own, as they gave saucepans, hairbrushes, dishes and tables cursory but possessive glances. Sometimes there were smiles. It was the glass of tatty stuffed parrots which drew bargain hunters. Inexpert fingers fumbled the keys of the rosewood cottage pianoforte, the instrument to which Mary had fondly retreated for hours every day when at home. 'No', she thought, an auction was not a sale, it was an humiliation; like being pilloried in stocks in the old market square when punishments were public.

Mary remembered going to a sale with Mamma once. She had bought an amazing amount of kitchen paraphenalia. Poor Mamma, if she had a vice it was an inability to miss what appeared a bargain. 'Well, dear, it just might come in handy', she would rationalize. A lot of furniture, after all, was an economy as its bulk left less bare square footage to heat. Bidding at auctions for Mamma was compulsive — like a gambler on a roulette wheel. 'Spending money again to save money', Papa would groan after Mamma had indulged her dreaded going-going-gone fever. Now the whisk (which cut one's hands as it beat eggs), and a horrid pair of nutcrackers which had seemed irresistible at the time, were once again to go under the hammer.

Memories. Memories. Now everything not safe with the pawnbroker was being stripped from the Oxnams. Parishioners came that Friday to see Thomas Oxnam brought low in his sin and in his debts; to see the scattering of comforts bought with profits which many farmers had resented. The atmosphere before bidding began was tense. Mr Tremaine, the auctioneer, whom everyone knew so well — 'one man's bargain is another man's loss' was a homily of which he was fond — banged his worn hammer on the table for silence. The light-hearted chatter died down and at precisely 2 o'clock on the last Friday in April the sale — the farewell — of the Oxnam home began.

The Oxnams had decided to go to Queensland and the *City of Agra*, on which the Queensland Agent-General had booked their passages, was to sail three days later from London. They would leave Newlyn the next day.

The auctioneer started. 'Now ladies and gentlemen what am I bid for these fine feather mattresses? One pound for an opening bid. I am bid one and two; one and three shillings; one and four shillings to Mr Pearce; one and five shillings... two pounds. Going, going, going to — No two and one. Gone to Mr Pearce!'

The proceeds from this sale were not going to be high. Mary slipped away. She walked, then she almost ran up the rainswept hillside. She looked down at the house; the land was no longer theirs, but she did not feel apart from it. This little bit of Cornwall would always be in her heart. One day she would return to this land which had given them from less to less, to nothing.

On Saturday, the Feast Day of the village patron, St Newlyna, who had figured as a backdrop to their lives, the Oxnams left Cornwall forever. It is worse to leave a home in England in winter, for at the end of the day when the night and cold are shut out a special sense of home comes when the fire soars and warms. But at last the grate was empty and the Oxnams gave up sorting through the jumble of not only 6,000 more days of Mamma and Papa's marriage but also Grandfather's life: orange boxes, washed jam jars, odd collar studs, balls of used string, the unsold butter churn, rusty mousetraps, half-filled earthenware jars of flour and sugar, overflowing button jars, odd bootlaces. Much that might have proved useful was now demoted to rubbish. Government-sponsored migrants could take so little on the crowded ships. It had been a heartbreaking job for Mary to choose what possessions would continue in her life. 'A little self-denial', was the phrase she repeated as flames leapt around the words of old diaries, letters and souvenirs — the dance programme with the blue ribbon from the Hunt Ball, rough copies of letters to London, applications for a post — until they were all ashes. She tore the favourite pages out of cherished books too bulky to take, but gleefully threw away the newspaper cutting reporting on the formation of the Women's Emigration Society:

In Australia there is a deficiency of women, as there is a superabundance on this side of the globe... The Bishop of Queensland guaranteed that women of a superior class going to that colony should meet with a hearty welcome from ladies there, and receive every possible help on their first landing. It was pointed out that ladies at the outset must not shrink from undertaking work that might seem a little beneath them... But few women are free of ties so we must look for orphan governesses, orphan lady-nurses, orphan milliners, apprentices, orphan hands in manufacturing establishments, or orphan servant maids... Surely 'fresh air' and 'freedom' are words which judiciously reiterated will stir young minds. For the little maid-servant in the Australian bush, although she will have to work hard, will enjoy her share of freedom and the new and less conventional life...

The article stressed the lack of educated women in the colonies:

Their presence is needed to soften and refine colonial life. Men of culture who were emigrants wanted to look for wives among women of their own class, not as they were now often compelled to do, among domestic servants... If only bone and muscle emigrates, the tone of the colony must deteriorate... There is plenty of work for cultivated women emigrants as governesses, if they did not disdain to be useful...

Handbills were to be distributed through young women's bible classes, the Governesses' Benevolent Institution, the Metropolitan Association for Befriending Young Servants, the Association for the Higher Education of Women... and at the doors of factories.

As Mary went through her things for the very last time she put in the bluebells dried between pages of her bible. If they had not had to forsake their belongings, their home, if everything had been theirs to come back to, then Mary would have been very happy to visit Australia. After all, it was exciting. But migrating meant interrupting so much in her life. Perhaps by a miracle she would not help to remedy the defeciency of females in Queensland and she would stay at Nanhellon. Perhaps a man would appear with money for a prize bull sold by Papa years ago, or a telegram would announce the inheritance of a fortune from a distant relation. At moments, though, Mary felt pleased to leave the village gossips. No, perhaps she would be at Nanhellon next week when the potatoes were raked and the sheep were tailed, and they would hear the first cuckoo herald spring. Hopefully, they would no longer hear Mamma trying to soothe the children by misquoting Shakespeare, 'Sweet are the uses of adversity, ugly as a toad is their venom...' Mamma had a ready quote, either from the bible or Shakespeare, for every misfortune.

Papa had gone ahead with the heavy luggage. He had taken the advice in a guide book on Queensland: 'A galvanized iron tank is of inestimable value in the dry climate, and costs little or no freight', instructed the writer. 'It can be filled with articles not required on the voyage and makes an excellent packing-case.'

Mary stood on the doorstep and looked out across the field to the disused mine. Idly she stripped the bark from a dormant twig of jasmine. She listened to the rural noises — a rook cawing, a sheep bleating — and spoke no word to her brothers and sisters but walked slowly and evenly to the end of the gravel path, to the white wooden gate, to the waggon waiting on the road, then she turned and stepped carefully back again to the dark green front door — a last touch: 'That was our house'. In the same mechanical fashion she retraced her steps to the fowlyard. The hens, of course, had already gone on their journey. Like the pet donkey. It was all over now. Goodbye. Goodbye forever and forever.

'The waggon is far too crowded for us, too heavy for the horses', thought Mary. Then off they went. Suddenly. They left their home standing in its amiable fields. The road narrows and winds so much on the descent from the village to Nanhellon that it would be calamitous for two carriages to meet. They held their breaths as

they went up for the last time. They left the village. They left the church with its ominous fig tree, still bare of leaves, they left Grandfather slumbering in his grave. Near the fig tree the blacksmith's sons ran to and fro across the road with a balloon. A pig had been slaughtered; they had waited until it had been bled, gutted and quartered, to be given the bladder washed of its pungent urine. Blown up with the veins running through it, like a map on a string, the bladder was the primitive ancestor of balloon and football — the bladder of the Elizabethan fool. And that was Mary's last picture of Newlyn.

When the Oxnams got to Truro Station groups of townsmen, of low class, sat round stiffly on benches. All of them wore their best clothes and hats; all of them were for the train to London, to journey to a new life, a new land. Each family remained separately huddled on the station. The Cornish motto 'One and All' did not lend a feeling of solidarity that morning, but some of them with forced bonhomie were hoping that it was a happy day, the prelude to ease and plenty; it was the weather and the wages that they looked forward to. These were proud men, men who had avoided the workhouse or parish charity.

When the train came farewells were brief in case they missed the whistle and missed their new life. The tears, though, lingered. Arms entwined briefly, shoulders hastily clapped, kisses exchanged, 'God bless you', said with trembling lips. Goodbye. Goodbye. And the train was off, slowly at first, to London.

Mary's carriage was not a padded saloon with chocolate-coloured cloth compartments, wicker hat-rails, ornate oil-lamps; nor did it have those languid first-class passengers — high-collared ladies with tartan shawls, wine-flasks and copies of *The Times*. Papa said it wasn't the hardness of travelling third class, it was the smell of the cheap eau de colognes mixed with that of the unbathed labourers that he could not bear. The Oxnams were in one of the cheapest compartments on the train; a worn, dusty, drafty, plain wood carrriage.

Various colonial emigration schemes had endured in fits and starts. Some Australian colonies paid the emigrants' fares to London, as well as their passages to Australia, charging nothing for the trip which cost between £20 and £30 a head. Queensland and South Australia at that time paid the total cost for many emigrants, even providing them with bedding, while Victoria covered some fares but made a small charge for bedding and utensils needed on the voyage. Cornish miners, known as Cousin Jacks abroad, had established themselves in great numbers in South Australia since the 1840s where they manned and managed the copper mines. Now Queensland wanted expert immigrants to mine the minerals dormant under her earth.

As always Mary was reading. On the way up to London she re-

read one of Charles Dickens's articles about 'going' and was thankful she was not sailing from Southampton:

> Southampton is now the great port of embarcation for Government emigrants from the south coast... emigrants are temporarily housed and fed at the London Emigration Depot at the Nine Elms Station... the extensive suite of lofty well ventilated rooms, once the London headquarters of the Company, are now converted into dormitories, refectories, and reception rooms for Government emigrants... At Southampton the disused terminus contains a hundred beds for married couples; the secretary's rooms accommodate single men; and single women are safely accommodated in the old treasury... The savoury fumes of soups and meats permeate the whole establishment... The humble passengers begin to pour in... hopeless confusion...
>
> They who have been inured to labour are off, from hunger, toil and sorrow, to plenty, to comfort and happiness. They are off, from the poorhouse, the jail, and the asylum, to the green hills, and fertile fields of a new land.

More depressing were hints for emigrants in the article 'What to Take to Australia':

> It is well for a family party to have just enough to enable them to enter the first suitable empty house in Melbourne or Sydney, and commence housekeeping at once, with a trunk for a seat and tea-chest for a table... Every party of not less than four should take a small three-pole tent without the poles. A workman may take his tools — a digger a navvy's spade, a pick, and a heavy crowbar... On board ship any old trowsers... Shoes without heels...
>
> In the colonies waterproof boots are a mistake; the water comes in at the top, and stays there until let out by a hole. In the Bush, and at the Diggings, woollen Jerseys, blue or red, are the wear, and blue-striped shirts...
>
> The following is the lowest scale of outfit required by the Government commissioners from free passengers: For males: six shirts, six pairs stockings, two ditto shoes, two complete suits of exterior clothing. For Females: six shifts, two flannel petticoats, six pairs stockings, two ditto shoes, two gowns. Towels and soap. And they supply each emigrant, in return for the deposit of one or two pounds, with a mattress, bolster, blankets, counterpane, canvas bag, knife, fork, and drinking mug.
>
> In the Family Colonisation Society's ships closets are provided with cisterns, pumps, and taps... Each passenger is also required to provide the following articles: knife and fork, table and tea spoons, metal plate, hook pot, drinking mug, water-can, washing-basin, two cabbage nets, one scrubbing brush, half a gallon of sand, half a bath-brick, two sheets of sand-paper, two coarse canvas aprons, hammer, tacks, leather straps with buckle to secure the beds neatly on deck when required to be aired, three pounds of marine soap...
>
> A wicker-covered stone or glass bottle will be found handy for keeping the supply of water. Thirst is better removed by washing out the mouth and lips than by drinking, when water is scarce... In the tropics, the children are constantly crying for drink.

At intervals, as Mary turned the pages of Dickens's old maga-zine, she looked through misty panes of glass, ignoring the travel-lers with their picnics of salted pilchards, potato pasties and saffron buns. The express took twelve hours to travel the 279 miles from Truro to Paddington; many passengers were restless and cold. Mary watched the bleak moorland pass, windswept acres bereft of trees; the last of the wild expanse of Bodmin Moor. Clay dumps rose from the River Fal to Lostwithiel; the waters ran milky white.

Many passengers sang old Cornish songs. A few yards, past the end of Brunel's thirty-four viaducts near Saltash, a few more inches, and the train would move them off Cornish soil forever. The train went slowly as it crossed the 455 feet of iron bridge which spans the River Tamar border linking the Celts with the English. Goodbye Cornwall. Goodbye forever and forever. Over the bridge. They were on land which had always been foreign. No more toasts of 'Fish, Tin and Copper'; no more tall mine chimneys smoking; no more men shouldering pickaxe and a meagre wage on bent backs. For a moment Mary saw the children near the church of St Newlyna run-ning, running with the pig's bladder blowing in the breeze, faster, faster until the string broke and the bladder flew up high above the church and disappeared. Now she was homeless, a wandering emig-rant seeking a better land; the hope of the country to come. Other refugees from the Truro district, also to cross the seas in the *City of Agra*, had been attracted by the Queensland Government's adver-tisement in the *Royal Cornwall Gazette*. The *Gazette* had also published legal notices advising Thomas Oxnam's creditors to apply to the solicitor for payment, and the auction notices for the Oxnam farm and furniture. Even the strangers on the train knew how close Papa had come to bankruptcy.

The sound of wheels and charge of steam broke the silence of that cold spring day, the day of St Newlyna. The train went on and on, further away from the ancient church tower, from what till yester-day was home, onward to something remote, a place with a different climate and government but, like England, pink on the map, still part of Queen Victoria's Empire. The roaming had begun. On they went past Plymouth, past Devonport and its Royal Albert Bridge where warships were being refitted. Devon seemed to Mary to be un-friendly. Somerset, Wiltshire, Buckinghamshire, Windsor Castle away over on the left with the flag flying as Queen Victoria was in residence. Then Langley Station, famed since the Great Western Railway Company's battle with Eton College authorities. It was too dark to see Mr Tickler's jam factory at Southall. London's Padding-ton at last. Just the magnificently horsed bus to the ship which would take them to the antipodes where no one would know about the Oxnams. Queensland was the final place for a fresh start.

Chapter Six

Mr Micawber's Solution

Afterwards Mary remembered little of London; events had moved too fast and her heavy eyelids had been drooping with weariness that night. But she caught the feeling of bustle, the glow of gas lights, the din of the hackney carriages, the roads paved with cobblestones and bricks that lead down between huge warehouses to the water's edge. Men shouted from heavy drays and yelled as they pushed hand carts. Thousands of anchored ships, some with funnels, others with sails, formed streets on water. The *City of Agra*, a three-masted windjammer built in Liverpool the year that Mary had been born, was an early iron clipper; a pretty little ship with a lot of overhang forward and raking masts and a highly coloured part-angel, part-woman figurehead on the prow.

Although the *City of Agra* was similar to the *Cutty Sark* in size — being 213 feet long, 34 feet wide, 20 feet deep and also with two decks and poop, plus top gallant forecastle — unlike that famous ship which beat all-comers through the foul Cape Horn passage, the *Agra* never broke sailing records on runs between the Motherland and the Australian colonies. She was fast, though. The Nova Scotia crew would take 'the old girl' nonstop to Queensland in about eighty to ninety days.

It was late and very dark that long Saturday night when a three-oared boat plied backwards and forwards to load the last of the 317 passengers, both steerage and saloon, on board. All day the thirty crew had been busily engaged in coiling ropes, spreading out sails to dry and storing in the hold baggage not wanted on the voyage. The *Agra* had been almost instantly changed overnight; for the outward journey the grain holds had been converted into dormitories with

59

The City of Agra *(National Maritime Museum)*

hammocks and bunks for passengers. Mary was put with her two sisters into the unmarried women's section.

It was a blurred memory of a scene from *David Copperfield*. Between decks, the emigrants, all with free or assisted passages, looked around forlornly; now they were afloat; English soil was gone. Homeless and dispossessed they had taken Mr Micawber's solution, a ship to Australia. Now here were the nine Oxnams, aged from two to forty-two, the *'nouveaux pauvres'*, mingling with the working classes; their common cause was to create a New World, where the inconveniences of the Old would not exist. There were miners, shopkeepers, coach-men, merchants, farmers, blacksmiths, tailors, labourers, fishermen, schoolteachers, twenty-one school-age children, plus the captain's wife. Now they were all to be 'mates' with no regard to class or privilege.

David Copperfield captured the horror of the migrant ships as he bade goodbye to Mr Micawber:

> It was such a strange scene to me, and so confined and dark, that, at first, I could make out hardly anything; but, by degrees, it cleared, as my eyes became more accustomed to the gloom, and I seemed to stand in a picture by Ostade. Among the great beams, bulks, and ringbolts of the ship, and emigrant-berths, and chests, and bundles, and barrels, and heaps of miscellaneous baggage — lighted up, here and there, by dang-

60

ling lanterns; and elsewhere by the yellow daylight straying down a windsail or a hatchway — were crowded groups of people, making new friendships, taking leave of one another, talking, laughing, crying, eating and drinking; some, already settled down into the possession of their few feet of space, with their little households arranged, and tiny children established on stools, or in dwarf elbow-chairs; others, despairing of a resting-place, and wandering disconsolately. From babies who had but a week or two of life behind them, to crooked old men and women who seemed to have but a week or two of life before them; and from plough-men bodily carrying out soil of England on their boots, to smiths taking away samples of its soot and smoke upon their skins; every age and occupation appeared to be crammed into the narrow compass of the 'tween decks...

Mary wanted to cry; constantly she was on the verge of tears. She found if she thought very hard of an iceberg and kept blinking that the tears would only fall inside her, into a secret hollow of sadness. 'Oh, God', she repeated to herself, 'Please, please make it easier for Papa, for all of us'. And then she would think of home, the cats and the hens, and her eyes would sting.

'Don't be unhappy', whispered Nellie. 'It's going to be better. Think of all the space and opportunity, Minnie.'

Mary interrupted. 'I did ask you all not to call me Minnie any-more. Please!' Mary's nickname of 'Minnie' was somewhat inappro-priate now that she had grown up and she pleaded with her family to call her Mary.

Dr de Touche, assisted by Mrs Gunn, the ship's matron, gave each passenger a medical examination. One man suspected of having a contagious disease was sent ashore. Rules were strict as both space and timing was tight on the windjammers. Speed was a matter of pride and survival for a clipper captain. The fastest and loveliest vessels the world had ever seen, the clippers were threat-ened in the late 1870s by grimy smoke-stacked steamships with their short-cut through the new Suez Canal. Sail, though, was still winning; five tons of British sailing ships countered every ton of steam. Also rivalry existed between captains who, in those cargo-racing heydays, were as celebrated as champion jockeys. Canvas was strained and cordage stretched to breaking point. Over half the world's commercial shipping flew the Red Duster, the flag of the British Merchant Navy. They carried an estimated 200,000 pas-sengers and as many seamen at any one time. It was the era of 'Britannia Rules the Waves'.

Once on board no passenger could go ashore, even though the *City of Agra* was delayed. On departure day, Monday, the sky was overcast and easterly gales made it cold and unpleasant. Captain Young waited for a westerly or south-westerly to take his ship down to the mouth of the Thames and into the English Channel. At last on Thursday 3 May a small steam tug towed the *Agra* through the forest of masts. The tug hooted and slowly pulled the ship from the quay, and the voyagers away from their past. It was an end. No scissors could have cut so quickly. Again it was the scene of Mr Micawber's departure: 'As the sails rose to the wind, and the ship began to move, there broke from all the boats three resounding cheers, which those on board took up, and echoed back, and which were echoed and re-echoed. My heart burst out when I heard the sound, and beheld the waving of the hats and handkerchiefs...'

On one wharf a small band kept up an incessant military march. The ship's siren blasted. The movement of the ships rushing to catch the westerly caused a wash and Mary for the first time heard the creaking noises on board, felt the lap of the water beneath them and the vague nausea caused by the sea's swell. As the sails were raised and spread to catch the wind, Mary joined the passengers crowded on the two rope-railed decks. The steam tug dropped its two ropes and they were, at last, in the maze of sands and tortuous channels of the Thames Estuary. Oh, what a splendid ship she was with brass a-glitter and a big sail area that made her fast in those light May winds.

Mary was full of joy one moment at the thought of how happy the family would be in the new land, and then ready to cry when she remembered that perhaps she would not again see England, see Cornwall, see Newlyn again. No, no, she would, she would come back. Return one day.

At Deal, where the Estuary, the Channel and the North Sea meet, the sea was crammed with merchantmen also waiting for a fair wind — more traffic between the Mother Country and the colonies. Sometimes up to 400 ships dotted the waters there. The *Agra*, too, had to wait; this time for two days for a headwind to take her down the Channel, the highway to the ocean.

After dawn on the third day, the gusts came, the Blue Peter was hoisted on the *Agra* and amid sudden action more sail was made and she glided past the white cliffs of Dover. By midday they had passed the last of the Seven Sisters where the Downs disappear into the sea. The barometer was falling.

The crowded noisy holds were too dim to read in so Mary took her book to the open deck. She could see the skies darken. The captain knew the signs all too well. If this kept up, his hopes to head southwest from the Isle of Wight to clip the corner of Brittany at Ushant would have to be altered. The weather-vane shifted as the strong Atlantic swell heaved and surged beneath the bows of the *Agra*. The fair wind was no more. The next day and night were blurred with sea-sickness, the oppressive intimacy of the dormitory, trying to lather marine soap with salt water to wash in. 'Come on, come along', said the matron as Mary lay on her bunk. Every passenger in health had to rise and roll up their beds at 7 a.m. unless otherwise permitted by the surgeon, and not roll them out again until after supper, which was served at six. Everyone had to be tucked up and silently in their bunks at 10 p.m. So, Mary spent much of her day in *her* area, huddled up on a wooden stool near her bunk.

The Lizard from Penolver Rocks (Royal Institution of Cornwall)

Mary mastered the art of undressing and dressing modestly in the dormitory. Every article of clothing taken off was delicately folded and neatly put at the end of her bed, and taken out and put on with equal care and punctiliousness in the morning. English boarding schools were supposed to inure a pupil for any hardship, for schools provided physical toil, self-discipline and the art of self-confident authority. But nothing, thought Mary, except poverty, could prepare you for living steerage on a sailing ship. The woman on the adjacent bunk did not even have a nail-brush, sponge or corset!

On the fifth day at noon, just before dinner at 1 p.m., Mary joined Nellie on deck. She was feeling better. In the distance rose a grey mass of rock which she recognized.

'Look, look, it's Start Point', she yelled. It was good to see a familiar landmark. This headland lies on the southernmost corner of Devon and she had once picnicked amongst its reddish brown rocks on a school outing. By late afternoon they were making for The Lizard — and the end of safe waters.

The ship passed a rough night as the blustering wind moved round to the south-west. Before Mary woke, the nightwatchman spotted the lighthouse off Lizard Point, the final sight of England for sailors leaving the Channel and entering the Atlantic. It is

63

England's southernmost point; no man in Britain can go farther south than The Lizard or travel to so grim a coast; waves here have eroded massive cliffs, destroyed boats by the hundreds and drowned men by the thousands.

Mary now watched anxiously. For the last hour on the bridge Captain Young and his first lieutenant had been intently surveying the barren shore through binoculars. Sometimes the captain went into the chart room. The sharp rocks were such a hazard to shipping that before the lighthouse was built on the end of the promontory in 1752, a coal fire had been kept flaming. Mary heard a fog signal drone on, warning the *Agra* to keep away from menaces unseen.

Mary looked for the signalling station at The Lizard, world famous for exchanging messages with every passing vessel. The Cornish, though, say that the place has other messages; it is a haunted area; a home for ghosts. Names of the inlets were reminders of past visitations of the devil — Halzephron, Cliffs of Hell, Devil's Bellow. At Gunwalloe the bells rang out from the tiny chapel on the rocks below, tolling for The Lizard phantoms. Behind there, beyond the cliffs, lay Pistol Meadow. Although only thirty miles inland, Newlyn East with its sunny green fields, church, and what until last week had been theirs, was beyond reach.

The barometer was still falling steadily, and the wind veering to the west. It would blow harder before the day was out. The ship plunged. The lights of The Lizard, of home, of those cosy firesides, fused into something past. England behind. Home behind. Debts, unpaid coal bills, friends and gossips behind. Superstitions, curses and the fig tree behind. Afloat and away. The passengers stood there on the deck, Anglo-Saxon and Celt, until nothing could be seen but sea, ships and sea-gulls. Outward-bound forever. Leaning on the roped-rail, clutching her bonnet and shawl, Mary sniffed back a few tears. 'How many of us will ever see England again?' she thought as she watched the land fast disappearing. Now they were on what they had looked at all their lives, the water they had touched so often after coaxing Grandfather, 'Come on, one more hill and we'll be on the sea'. The land got dimmer and dimmer. It was time for their lunch of pea-soup, boiled beef and plum pudding.

A tabby cat ran across the deck. Mary remembered the dreadful Thursday when Papa had gathered up the excess feline members of the household — fifteen in all — put them in three sugar sacks and taken them to Truro and let them loose on ships in the river. 'Every ship needs ratters and mousers', he had explained, adding that cats liked the motion of waves. Now Fluff, like the Oxnam cats, dog and donkey were scattered; quarantine regulations in Queensland limited the entry of animals, while legislation governed the entry of people. It wanted to be a select colony.

Ten days after leaving London the *Agra* passed between the Azores and Madeira, 'running her Eastings down'. The Cape of

A ship aground at The Lizard (Royal Institution of Cornwall)

Good Hope came next and then across the Pacific, catching the currents to Queensland.

The ship was crowded, every berth was occupied. Mary wrote in her diary: '... miserable. Whatever I do, whatever folly I commit, I will not take another sea voyage.' She was two decks down in a dormitory lit only with swaying smelly oil lamps, candles being forbidden because of the fire risk. The bunks were just stretchers of wood and a ticking stuffed with straw. On some of the ships, each group of a dozen passengers or so formed a mess and cooked and shared their meals. But on this journey the *Agra* had a small galley crew. The food was awful, and as it got worse as the fresh provisions were finished, the wooden nutmeg grater and pepper pot disguised its flavour.

The Atlantic was rainy and tempestuous but with gunwales

awash, making sixteen knots at least, they were driven, canvas tearing, booms snapping, to the limits the iron hull would stand. Again it took courage for Mary to rise from her upper berth and go to the mess-tables. The sight of porridge and kippered herring was sickening and she went and sat on the stool marked Oxenham which her father had managed somehow to buy. Papa said, 'Jolly clerk writing all that paperwork so we could switch countries misspelt our name. We're all Ox-en-hams now.'

Mary, however, thought that Papa had deliberately changed the spelling so as to identify them with John Oxenham, the Devon man, who with Drake had been the first Englishman to see the Pacific, and who had defended Britain against the Spanish. Also, perhaps Papa wanted to lose a few people — and bills.

As Mary sat on deck, spray came up every few minutes and wet the book she was reading as well as herself. She turned away at the sight of people drinking mugs of half-cold beef-tea with grease spots floating on the top.

The rules on board ship were numerous and strict: every passenger had to attend breakfast from 8 to 9 a.m., dinner at 1 p.m. and supper at 6 p.m.; on each passenger deck three safety lamps were to be lit at dusk and kept burning all night; one lamp to be placed at each of the hatchways used by the passengers; the passengers when dressed were to sweep the decks (including the space under the bottom of their berths), and to throw the dirt overboard; breakfast not to commence till this is done. The sweepers for the day to be taken in rotation from the males above fourteen years, in proportion of five for every 100 passengers. Duties of the sweepers: to clean the ladders, hospitals, round-houses and waterclosets, to pump water into the cisterns or tanks for the supply of the waterclosets, to sweep the decks after every meal, and to dry, holystone and scrape them after breakfast. Beds to be well shaken and aired on deck, and the bottom boards to be removed and dry-scrubbed and taken on deck, at least twice a week. Two days in the week to be appointed by the master as washing days, but no clothes on any account to be washed or dried between the decks; the coppers and cooking vessels to be cleaned every day. The hatches to be kept open (weather permitting) at all hours; no gunpowder or loose hay or straw to be taken on board by any passengers. No smoking allowed between decks; all immoral or indecent acts or conduct, blasphemous or obscene language, swearing, gambling, drunkenness, or insubordinate conduct, are strictly prohibited; firearms, swords and other offensive weapons, as soon as the passengers embark, to be placed in the custody of the master. No sailor to remain on the passenger deck among the passengers except when on duty; no passenger to go to the ship's cookhouse without special permission from the master, nor to remain in the forecastle among the sailors on any account...

The degradation of travelling steerage cut Papa deep. How he envied the fare-paying passengers in the more comfortable parts of the ship with the captain and the captain's wife, Mrs Young. He swallowed humiliation whenever he saw the name Thomas Oxenham on the rota. Down went his knees and he scrubbed like a common labourer's wife with those hands which before had hardly held anything except the reins of his horse, a rifle, or the lead of a bull. Worse was the total prohibition on alcohol; no nips of whisky to help him sleep through the snores, grunts and whispers of the other couples in the dormitory, or to soften the embarrassment of sleeping with his dear wife in what was after all a public room.

'And the bible tells us that Timothy took a drop of wine', Papa complained.

The interpretation of the bible was another sore point for passengers. The religions represented on board were numerous: Church of England, Roman Catholic, Congregationalist, Methodist, Jew, Presbyterian and atheist. Yet on Sunday they all had to attend the service read by Captain Young. Rule 8 stated: '... the passengers to be mustered at 10 a.m. when they will be expected to appear in clean and decent apparel. The day to be observed as religiously as circumstances will admit...'

Elizabeth McSwiggin, the only passenger who did not endure the salt beef and waves, had been a Roman Catholic, but words from the Church of England prayer book were read as the bell tolled and her body, wrapped in a Union Jack, was slipped into the Atlantic. Her husband was unsure of her blessed resurrection because the service had been from the wrong religion.

Mary passed three months on this small floating island in the company of 315 fellow migrants, each day as dreary as the last. Boredom when carried to this degree leads to quarrels, depressions and petty arguments, such as the fuss over Miss Jones's hat-box. Steerage was divided into three dormitories so that married couples, single men and single women could be segregated and the later watched over by matron. Rules governed what each passenger was allowed to have in the dormitory and Mary could not understand how Miss Jones's hat-box had gone unnoticed. Miss Jones slept in the next berth and the blessed box blocked up the floor and Mary kept falling over it when she sat on the floor to pull her small case from under her berth. No one else had a hat-box!

And frequently Miss Jones came on deck smelling of Mary's tooth powder; the special one for travelling that Miss Moore had given her as a farewell present, together with the nutmeg grater. The grater had vanished. Mary had reported its loss to matron and then, horror upon horrors, she had found it in the pocket of her coat! How could she tell matron without sounding petty or like a sneak?

Sometimes it seemed that for ever more they would be jammed up in this ship, dashing through the endless sea, balancing their bodies to the sway and the reel, hearing the groan of the tackle and the swish of the sails, as the wind beat them on and on. Always there was the sea, endless, hostile, deep, ever-waiting below them. It was not just a voyage across the world, it was a voyage into the universe. As they moved over the dark waters, over the deep hidden currents, Mary looked to the sky, to the stars. When she looked back it seemed that she had spent all her life in a room, a pleasant room, but a only room, and now the door had been opened and she was entering the world, into whatever was beyond. Sometimes she seized the new moment and tried to hold it, but it was like trying to pick up water.

Mary tried to tell these thoughts to Fanny whom she had chummed up with. But when she translated them into sentences they sounded trite, cliched. Fanny had studied in Dresden until her father had thrown himself under a train at Waterloo Station when he was to be bankrupted, and the lack of finances had forced her to return to England. When playing Chopin at a neighbour's house a few weeks after her father's funeral, a guest had asked to escort Fanny home. No, her maid would accompany her, she had retorted. Determined, the suitor visited Fanny's mother the next day. He had been to Australia in the goldrush and was returning to open a general store in Charters Towers, Queensland. Fanny's mother, desperate, accepted his proposal on behalf of her eighteen-year-old daughter. Now Fanny was an unhappy bride, although a little comforted by the company of her younger brother, Joseph, who was with her on the ship.

Fanny and the Oxnams were not alone in their worlds of grief. Everyone on board had suffered some form of alienation, for that is the effect of most migration. The voyage was more than a journey; it was a period of transition. No regular passenger journey then was longer than the voyage to the antipodes. Australia was not only the last continent discovered by Westerners, it was the most distant from Europe. After eighty to ninety days in cramped and difficult conditions, some wounds were healed, some old ways lapsed. There was time to forget and to adapt to the nautical surroundings and to people on board. If set down in a land of strangers after a few days or a week at sea, still with all the old habits, grievances and ideas of home, the shock of trying to live in another country would have been greater.

On 24 May, cheers were raised on the occasion of Queen Victoria's birthday. It was remembered during the birthday celebrations that Victoria was now, since 1 January, Empress of India. The ship had been called after a distinguished city in India, famous because of the Taj Mahal. This ship, though, was not destined to call in to India. Steamers refuelled at coaling stations set up in distant parts of the globe, but clippers needed no fuel and paused for nothing. Food was

68

salted, pickled and rationed so they could sail non-stop without having to pick up more supplies. How tantalizing it was for Mary; distant coasts, the green of foreign lands, were dimly seen, in moments they were past mountains, towns and beaches. The anchor was never dropped, the sails were never furled as on and on they sailed.

At last the waves got warmer and the sea calmer. Pitch in the seams of the decks bubbled; the sun was a great glare and it was so hot that Mary and Nellie splashed saltwater over each other. Then came a dead calm. The ocean was as smooth as a mirror, not a ripple to be seen on it. The old empty matchbox that Mary dropped overboard did not move from the side of the *Agra*. Every now and again the sails flapped against the masts while the ship rolled slowly from side to side. The heat was intense and terrible; there was no shade; the decks and holds were airless, like furnaces; drinking water in the tank was almost boiling. Passengers restlessly trying to find cooler places found that in a ship in a tropical calm they don't exist. Then, suddenly, God answered the prayers for a wind to take them on. Mary heard Captain Young's voice on the loud hailer. 'All hands shorten sail!' Up the rigging the crew swarmed like ants, some throwing themselves into the tops, others ascending the top-gallant yards and bravely running out to either yard-arm; the sailors on deck pulled and hauled. The topsails were quickly furled. Scarcely had the sailors descended when Mary, who with other passengers had been ordered below, heard the loud roar of waves.

'Down for your lives!' yelled the Captain.

Wind struck the *Agra* and drove her down. Over she heeled. Down, down, she went. Then up on the crest of a wave. The sea ran mountains high. As storm waves tossed them into the air and under waves, it wasn't just nausea that gripped Mary, it was a new fear: death. Water streamed into the berths below as families huddled together, touching, holding each other for safety and comfort. As things quietened down passengers related harrowing stories of ships 'just like this': the crew of one ship had all been washed overboard and the passengers left floating forever on the sea until they 'perished to a man' because the lifebelts were rotten. Mamma reminded her brood, yet again, that if they fell overboard to tread water, relax their hands and pretend they were climbing stairs, until they were rescued.

For Mary, the voyage was an interruption in living. Hardly a passenger on board did not count the days on calendars and on fingers — how vexing it was when the meridian was crossed and a whole day was lost! Their new lives could not begin until the voyage was over, until they were moved further down the globe, down the world to Australia. Some emigrants day-dreamed for hours about returning to the Old Country as millionaires. Sewing, reading, taking vigorous constitutionals up and down the deck, scrubbing or complaining about the food, did not divert them from fantasies. The conceits of migrants were described by Mrs Micawber when she told David Copperfield:

> Mr Micawber is going to a distant country expressly in order that he may be fully understood and appreciated for the first time. I wish Mr Micawber to take his stand upon that vessel's prow, and firmly say, *'This country I am come to conquer!* Have you honours? Have you riches? Have you posts of profitable pecuniary emolument? Let them be brought forward. They are mine!'... I wish Mr Micawber to be the Caesar of his own fortunes... From the first moment of this voyage, I wish Mr Micawber to stand upon that vessel's prow and say: 'Enough of delay; enough of disappointment; enough of limited means. That was in the old country. This is the new. Produce your reparation. Bring it forward!'

Meanwhile Mary was chosen by Captain Young to give lessons to the under-twelves every morning. It was a pleasant task, though she was sure that the lessons were not for erudition but to keep the children occupied and out of the way. Education in England was not compulsory, although the Foster Education Act seven years earlier had set up elementary schools in villages where no non-ecclesiastical ones existed. Back in Newlyn, already there were plans to supersede the Oxnam School.

As the ship crossed the South Pacific, her owners in Melbourne and London, Messrs J. Coupland, W.B. McGavin and J. Blyth, were trading shares in the *Agra* as if she were real estate. Mary never knew about this, for there was no radio on board, nor did it affect her, or any of the other passengers. Messrs McGavin and Blyth both increased their share in the boat and a new shareholder, a Mr William Cummings of Hackney, bought out a third of John Coupland's share. Mary would have been cynical if she had known that to men such as these she was no more than a piece of paper, the basic commodity in a shipbroking deal. For in the 1870s the transport of souls to the antipodes was a profitable business.

At dawn on the 27 July, another human cargo arrived on the coast of Queensland. Once in the bay, the crew lowered the anchor on the knotted rope to allow the custom officers and doctors on board to check the crew and passengers. Queensland was attempting to keep out deadly diseases and epidemics, as well as illicit alcohol and other dutiable items. No one was spared the heavy duties — as high as twelve shillings per case of wine — whether they came from far away or from a sister state. These duties were used to defray the huge state deficit, a deficiency partly' created by lavish loans to transport future citizens from Europe.

Now that they were in Australian waters, Mary and the other 315 emigrants were immigrants; for he who is an emigrant at one end of a journey becomes an immigrant at the other. An emigrant leaves his native soil for a foreign land; an immigrant is a newcomer. But the passengers, unaware of their grammatical metamorphosis, were gripped with the excitement of arrival; the atmosphere was thick with anticipation, like a market-day morning and Christmas Eve together.

For some of these shifted souls the life ahead would be full of halcyon days, but for others, including Mary, it would be a hard struggle. Within three years she would find herself eeking out a frugal existence on a small island near the Great Barrier Reef. Then she would wonder what the family had gained from crossing the world. Australia, though, gave Mary more than Cornwall could have done: immortality. The story of her fight against adversity on Lizard Island made her a symbol of the conflict of the white pioneers against nature.

Chapter Seven

The Promised Land

The waves of the Pacific Ocean crashed into a high and rolling surf on a dangerous bar at the entrance of the River Mary. Although the day was blue-skied and calm, the channel between the broad sandbanks was rough so the *Agra* lurched as passengers, for the last time, moved around their bunks. The voyage had taken three months but afterwards Nellie told her children that it had lasted six months; it had seemed such a very, very long journey.

And that morning in July all passengers were so very glad it was nearly over. There was a feeling of real joy among the chatter, excitement and farewelling. It was announced that the passengers would probably be able to see land at 8 o'clock, with the result that everyone was on deck at seven to get the first sight of that wonderful place. The prospect of putting feet on dry land got everyone to fever pitch. Well-being overflowed into good resolutions, promises to keep in touch with new chums. No one, though, except a few servant girls, nominated migrants under contract to future employers, had firm addresses. Few families knew where they would be living or what they would be doing after they disembarked. So the addresses of friends of friends, the strangers for whom they carried burdens called Letters of Introduction, were exchanged. Busily passengers got themselves, their clothes, their luggage and their coiffures ready to meet Dickens's Land of Opportunity. As at the beginning of the voyage, and now at the end, they leaned on the rope-rail with excitement. The waiting was over. Soon, within a matter of days, they would be taking possession of the soil. The gold and minerals that had been lying around would be their very own; they would build cities, clear fields and plant gardens.

The River Mary is navigable the whole twenty-five miles from the sea to Maryborough for moderate sized ships so the *Agra* slowly floated down the wide and tortuous stream. Mrs Oxnam said it was a good sign and portent that Mary was on a river that shared her name. Mary smiled again. With the other passengers she gazed longingly at the shore, so close they could nearly touch it. After months of nothing but sea, distant hazy shores and each other it was indeed wonderful to look close up at a tree, a flower, a horse. How fresh was every sight and every sound. But what a disappointment! To an Englishman nothing at first is more dreary than the Australian landscape during a drought with gum tree after gum tree, all the same, tall, lank, dull green with thin foliage of narrow leaves. So different from the European forest, so different from the descriptions of Australia. The monotonous bush of eucalyptus was broken here and there with plantations of sugar cane, maize and crops which seemed unfamiliar. Mary smiled again and again. Australia, Australia, we have arrived.

A patch of ground stretched in front of her, dotted with trees. Every one of them was dead. Some raised skeleton branches, like grey claws; some had fallen and littered the landscape. It looked like a shell-blasted battlefield. The trees, gum trees, had been ringed — a deep groove cut round each trunk — so they would die and leave more space to grow more food. More space! Land seemed to stretch as far as one could see; surely a man would never come to the end of it.

Nearly a century had passed since the first convicts had arrived at Botany Bay, the six states — New South Wales, Queensland, Victoria, South Australia, Tasmania and Western Australia — were now separate colonies, each with its own London-sent governor, legislative assembly and customs dues. The governor reigned but did not govern. Common citizenship, common traditions and common love of English ways bound the colonies with the mother country and Empire. Despite an influx of Europeans to the gold-rushes, the population was 98 per cent British stock. All the colonies — with the exception of Western Australia — had been give self-government on domestic issues, although the Imperial Parliament in London retained jurisdiction over foreign policy. Queen Victoria, Mr Gladstone, and the Colonial Office in London had the final say in this remote pocket of the British Empire.

In one particular way Australia was to prove especially difficult to govern and manipulate. For there has always been one indispensable requirement for the white hegemony: water. Australia is the least-watered continent on earth. In Mary's time there was little irrigation so when the land was besieged by droughts, the disaster was enormous. Thousands of Europeans went to Australia in the latter half of last century in an attempt to establish an Eden on earth; many were to sink into lassitude and let hope take over from

Maryborough Wharves (John Oxley Library)

ambition, others were to die of starvation, thirst, spider or snake-bites or malnutrition; most were to retreat to the safety of dull city suburbs. Others wandered around the vast land, always moving for the last time, always searching, but when they looked back on their lives they realized that they had 'gone walkabout' like the Aborigine they had subjected.

The dry scenery and the day-dreaming were over. The gang plank was suspended between wharf and ship and men and women were scrambling for the shore — the passengers who had been safely borne across the Pacific, through storms, gales and calms, were now 'down-under'.

'You go first', Papa said to Mary. 'No, no let Mamma and you go first.'

Mary felt a hesitancy about leaving the vessel which had become a temporary home, to set foot on their new country. The moment of recoil passed. The joy of having got to a chosen goal, a destination, obliterated the fact that the gang plank led to homelessness. After some jostling Papa and Mary were the advance-guard of Oxnams to walk sedately across the planks to put their feet on the much awaited continent. By chance they would be the first of the family to die in Australia; Nellie, Martha, Carrie and Sidney would be dead within twenty-five years. But how could they know the fates that awaited them; they had such hope. The sun was shining, the sky was blue and a stalwart little fellow announced himself with, 'Pardon me, sir, are you Mr Thomas Oxenham?' Mr Crane from Tooth & Company's Meat Boiling Down Works whom Papa had written to had come to meet them. Mary noted his narrow forehead, greased straight hair with centre parting, reclining chin and well-cut suit. From his opportune stares and grins Mary realized that Mr Crane was one of the surplus bachelors, so often reported in the English press.

The wharf was a place of frantic activity as the *Agra* dispatched luggage speedily so she could catch the tide up the river and sail to Brisbane where the remaining 119 passengers would disembark. Then the berths would be dismantled and the holds again jammed with wool for the return trip to England. Passengers stood beside their well labelled trunks, guarding them with care, for within them was all they owned in this new world.

Mary was aghast at the sight of Aboriginal women swaying along the gutters of the wide street draped in what she was sure should be on a bed. Female Aborigines, she was told by Mr Crane, in the neighbourhood of white settlements were then compelled to wear a blanket distributed free of charge by an agent of the Colonial Government, to both wean them away from the unchristian habit of nakedness and save the morals of the whites. Mary stared.

They had the longest thinnest legs protruding from under their grubby apparel ever imagined possible on a human being. Their heads were small, their trunks slender but their noses and lips were wide. Behind the women a few sooty-brown men strayed along. Were these urbanized, thin, graceful men the fierce warriors who had murdered the shepherds thirty-five years earlier, thus preventing a settlement at Maryborough?

'Oh, of course, you've never seen a coloured chappie, before!' ventured Mr Crane. 'Quite a shock, eh!'

Mary thought that Mr Crane would never get them, their trunks and the waggon together. They lingered on the edge of the wharf near the street while he and Papa talked. The Oxnam boys tried to locate the iron tank used as part of their baggage allowance.

Although winter, the weather, like a perfect summer day in England, gave Mary a feeling of pleasure but her eyes, accustomed to the lush greens and blues of the sea, kept blinking at the dryness, the dust and the odd feeling of tremendous space. At last they got into a cab and Mary saw that Maryborough, then the second largest town in Queensland, was not beautiful. Broad, straight streets, running in parallel lines, cut the town into numerous smaller squares, forming what were called blocks which were in turn divided

Timber cutters, Cooktown

into about ten plots. These were sold by the government to new settlers who had put up shops, banks, even an auction mart, a concert hall, a newspaper printers, a magistrate's court, a prison, a pawnbroker and a great many pubs.

'What d'yer think of our wide streets, like?' the driver of the horse-drawn cab enquired, not waiting for a reply. 'Yer could eat a sandwich while yer walking from one side to the other.'

Some land, though, was covered by tree-stumps left when bush was cleared, a reminder that Maryborough had been a poor town, a straggling place, until the discovery of the Gympie goldfields nine years earlier. A port had been needed for gold and diggers so Maryborough had been awakened into a gaudy and busy life. The tramp of 10,000 men on horse or foot and the roll of drays with teams of bullocks had beaten a highway through the sixty miles of bush between the two centres.

The cabbie was pleased to tell the Oxnams every highlight of the gold-rush. Men had lighted pipes with pound notes, washed their faces with champagne and even clergymen had torn off their collars and joined in the mad stampede which was now, alas, over as every year the gold yield was less.

'Queensland's the colony of gold and sugar', he continued. 'No sugar cane, no rum.'

The Oxnams eventually arrived at their hotel at sunset, tired out. The hotel had a broad verandah, bat-wing doors at the bar entrance and sunlight was softened inside by green hanging blinds.

Mr Crane had booked them into the Commercial Hotel for four days. Papa hoped that Mr Crane's initiative was hospitality; that his firm was picking up the bill. Mamma was not so sure. 'Shouldn't you thank him in advance?' she said. Whenever the family were alone the question of the hotel bill was raised. When Papa had actually addressed Mr Crane with, 'By jove, nice of you to go to all this trouble with the hotel', Mamma said that it had sounded ambiguous. If money was the root of all evil, Papa philosophized, it was like the root of the potato, the best part of the plant.

The drovers had come to town, too. Mary heard rough voices, yarning about vain deeds of prowess, through the thin weather-board walls — a happy sound of excitement and laughter that never ceased. Then came a total hush. 'The men have gone down to the pub, the bar at the back of the hotel', said Mr Crane as they sat in creaky wicker chairs on the wide verandah that led from their hotel bedrooms. There were a number of other groups, a farmer or two, a few shopkeepers.

Floating sugar-mill and rum distillery 1860s (John Oxley Library)

'When a ship from England arrives the men find an excuse to get to town', blurted Mr Crane nervously.

Stories of ship-loads of female immigrants arriving in Swan River or Rockhampton to be met by bachelors lining the shores, each with a telescope and a speaking trumpet, bawling out offers of marriage, was, of course, an exaggeration, Mr Crane added. As he spoke, noise from the pub became louder; voices individually inaudible joined into a chorus. If in pursuit of women the men certainly did not make it obvious, Mary thought. She supposed that with such lonely lives all the talk inside them came out at once.

Mr Crane, indecisive, kept repeating, 'I really must be going', but he never actually departed. Mary and Nellie, longing to feel the comfort and privacy of hotel bedrooms and real beds, had to sit as he and Papa smoked huge cigars, drank local rum and talked long after the dinner of lamb chops, mashed potatoes and peas had been eaten. When he finally went, his departure was only temporary. 'I'll be seeing you tomorrow', he said warmly. 'I will get you *all* about ten. I'm sure the children will want to see the works as well. See what lies behind meat cubes you buy in England.'

'Mr Crane's being so nice to us, dear; it's clear he's rather taken by you', said Mamma, who had come into the girls' room to make sure they were ready. They weren't.

Inwardly bad tempered at going to the Boiling Down Works — Nellie had luckily won the chore of looking after Sidney, then a tearaway of two-and-a-half — Mary wanted to stay still and relish liberty, being free of ship's rules. Downstairs in the hotel lounge a piano beckoned; her hands took to chords and keys.

Mamma interrupted the waltz, 'It's after all essential — the hotel bill, dear, and the possibility of a position for Papa.' Land ownership was, of course, Thomas Oxnam's aim but he was desperate for a stopgap job.

'Obviously you'll be all right, Papa', said Mary. 'Mr Crane works in the office and must know what a respected cattle dealer you were in Truro. And he wouldn't have gone to so much trouble just responding to a Letter of Introduction.'

Thomas Oxnam's good humour had been aided with a few swift glasses of the local product after all those month's of abstinence. However, he was clearly worried. Queensland was suffering from an emigration surfeit. People without capital, many without proper trades, had immigrated by the thousands. The aim of many men was to leave manual labour and become respectable. So there were too many petty traders. The tropical paradise planned was so different from reality. Already the new Queensland government had millions of pounds of public debt. It turned out that men would rather speculate with land than cultivate it.

Although gold had lured settlers and provided the colony with capital, it had kindled the gambling spirit that now pervaded all classes. Men tried to succeed by lucky ventures, by audacious speculations, almost by swindling, rather than by effort and thrift. There were too many examples of swift fortune and rapid acquisition to make men feel a duty to plod on.

Mr Crane arrived. Thirteen minutes early. 'Ready to go?' he shouted as a greeting.

He took Mary's gloved hand to help her onto the buggy and engaged her in conversation the whole eight miles to the bend in the River Mary to what Mr Crane called 'the establishment'. Mr Crane is a bore, Mary decided. He took it for granted that it was interesting for them to hear every detail. And they had newly-received letters from Cornwall which they were longing to re-read.

'Over a hundred men are employed and their cottages form quite a little village', he said, pointing as they drove along the sun scarred road. 'The slaughter and boiling-down buildings are extensive. The steam engine that works the machinery could drive a ferry boat!'

They alighted, met other employees, walked on; Mr Crane talked. The sickening smell of the place assailed their nostrils; the groans and roars of bullocks mad at the smell of blood assailed their ears. The animals stamped and pushed to leap over each other, fences, railings, anything to escape death. 'We usually kill between 1,400 and 1,500 cattle a month. Depends on what supply there is', he continued and, glancing towards Papa, added, 'No cattle are fattened here, they're all purchased from dealers and stations around.'

That would be Papa's new position: procuring cattle fit ·for flavour only. Instead of buying the best cattle, buying the worst. The prospect of a regular wage, though, almost compensated for everything: even for the air inside the office which was also permeated with the overpowering stench of whole herds being boiled in vats. Mamma thought that Papa, so sensitive to odours, would faint. 'The place stank', was all he commented later though.

Next they were escorted into the killing yard. A blonde man wearing a blue open-necked shirt visible under a dirty white overall clutched a flat-edged spear in both hands. From his elevated platform he quickly lowered his instrument and struck the brown bullock at the back of his neck. Before the beast dropped to the ground the man's spear hit another animal pushed from behind.

'These bullocks are too tough for meat. Walked too far', said Mr Crane as they stood near a heap of dead beasts, some still twitching with life. 'They're boiled down for lard, the extract is shipped to England in huge tin cylinders where they are portioned and wrapped into meat and soup cubes', Mr Crane went on. 'They used to call it portable soup.'

The steam from cows and bulls in the pot enveloped their whole beings now. 'It takes forty pounds of meat to make one pound of_ extract. They boil the fat into tallow and make oil from the feet. The refuse meat and offal are given to pigs. The hide is tanned here. Yes, the horns and hairs are sold...'

79

This was the Oxnam salvation; Papa buying cattle which would end up as Lieberg's Extract of Meat in England. Queensland was a pastoral colony with huge distances; large mobs of cattle were being continually shifted from one station to another, or to ports.

Papa, warned to compare nothing to England as already Anglo-Australians were extremely proud of their adopted home, said in an effort to make conversation, 'It must be quite a job mustering hundreds of fat bullocks and taking them over a thousand miles of rough country?'

'Yeh', answered Mr Crane, with another swift grin at Mary. 'From daylight to dusk a drover's on horseback, hot weather, cold nights, rain and drought, he crawls along with his stock-whip and dog. The cattle's pace is so slow he's hardly movin' at all. They dawdle. Sometimes drover fellows go bonkers. It's the slow pace and the flies.'

The drought, disaster for the colony, was good business for the Boiling Down Works and for Thomas Oxnam in his new job; scrawny cattle were going cheap. Animals were rushed to slaughter before they died. No wonder John Campbell had established the first Boiling Down Works there at the end of the Great Drought in the early 1840s.

The Oxnam family had a weatherboard house on the bend of the river near other employees. Wooden steps lead to a wide wooden verandah under an overhanging corrugated iron roof. A picket fence, covered in peeling white paint, marked their plot. At night the Oxnams sat outside on creaking wicker chairs — just like the ones at the hotel — and listened to the shrill of the cicadas. They always sat on the verandah in the dark because the lantern attracted dreadful mosquitoes, so virulent near water. But it was good being on the river; the boys made money by wriggling their feet in mud at low tide — crabs caught on their toes were sold for a penny each. After a while none of the Oxnams really smelt the odour from the nearby Boiling Down Works; not really.

Chapter Eight

A Double~barrelled Name

'One day, dearest, you will fathom it all', was all Papa could say. Thomas Oxnam was now a worn-out man, his large eyes full of sorrow. His hand shook slightly as it lay on Mary's shoulder. She moved away, flung herself down on her knees beside the wooden steps of the verandah and burst into a passion of weeping. His favourite person, his eldest child, she had found out...She would never truly trust him again. There was nothing he could say, nothing. He turned pale and his lip trembled. The man that fathers an illegitimate child can offer only love as reparation for the shame. It was a shaming thing for Mary now.

'The trouble is that I'm not really an Oxnam', she cried after seeing the birth certificate needed for an application for the school she was trying to set up.

'My name is Phillips; in England the child always takes its mother's name. Perhaps you could legally adopt me Papa?' she uttered with sarcasm. Her father bowed his head sadly. His eyebrows and sideburns were already peppered with grey.

The words went round in her mind: fornicator, fornicator... illegitimate, illegitimate...bastard, bastard... born out of wedlock, born out of wedlock...

She could feel herself dramatize her situation; she was also cross with her mother for being a loose woman, although she discouraged ill thoughts, even temporary ones, about poor Mamma. Papa, after all, should have done the decent thing and married her before the birth. Then her thoughts veered in the opposite direction: poor Papa having to get married, having to be married seventeen years to a woman he wouldn't have married otherwise. Or would he?

She remembered the scene, earlier that day, when the official in the government office had said 'Phillips?' and she had replied, 'No, Oxnam! I mean Oxenham.' For she hadn't bothered to read the certificate properly, not beyond the birth date. The only course was to pretend that Mamma had been married previously to a Mr Phillips. Widowed when young. Mary called herself Mary Phillips-Oxenham from that day onwards. It was less suspicious if she did not hide the other name, in case the birth certificate followed her around.

Oh why, oh why did Papa wait for nearly a year after her conception to marry Mamma? She counted backwards on her fingers; she was born on 17 January 1860... No, no, it couldn't be true. She covered her face with her hands. She had been conceived, she couldn't bear to say it, even to herself. Oh, perhaps she had been conceived on May Day? She would try and get enough courage to ask Mamma — how, though, could she talk about such a delicate, intimate subject?

Papa, she realized gleefully, had no legal control over her. By law he was her step-father. She longed to assert herself against him, but, at the same time, was ashamed of herself even day-dreaming about such satisfactory revenge.

The drought got worse. Streams disappeared into parched earth, grass turned brown and vanished; sometimes the knees of cattle gave way as they struggled through mud to the waters of some fast-evaporating pool. Papa went out to shoot the kangaroos with Mr Crane, who had now given up his role as Mary's suitor. The kangaroos, he explained, had to go. They were pests, ready to devour any grass or crop that the sun had not shrivelled.

The Marsupial Act, recently passed to encourage the destruction of kangaroos, meant there was a government reward for each hide. After all, it wasn't cruel; the kangaroos were eating up every blade of grass and would starve out cattle and sheep. The hunt wasn't for sport — gentlemanly codes were forgotten — it was for survival. Two wings of men on fast horses widened out over a plain; at a signal, the assault began. Horses, Aboriginal trackers, dogs, rushed in, forcing the kangaroos finally into a fenced trap — wide at the opening to take in the dozens of pests and narrowing into a V. Once trapped, the slaughter began. The Aborigines knocked them senseless with tomahawks and clubs. It wasn't cruel, the farmers reiterated, just look at the dead livestock. There wasn't enough grass for both.

The land distant from the town was like the Valley of the Shadow of Death, strewn with the skeletons and decaying carcasses of wretched animals, perished from starvation and thirst. Horses, cattle, sheep, kangaroos, emus and koala bears lay dead in all directions, tainting the air and attracting crows and magpies who picked at the flesh. Desolation was relieved here and there by weird drought-resistant shrubs with salty leaves and insulated roots.

Agricultural settler's house 1860s (John Oxley Library)

'The good years give an erroneous idea of the grazing capabilities of the land', a colonial office employee told Papa when he applied for his share of this paradise where there was 'an acre for everyone'. The price of crown land seemed to range from nothing to five shillings an acre, with ten years to pay. Men who had been penniless all their lives could be, but seldom were, the lords of vast estates, territorial magnates. It was not enough, however, to claim land and leave a manager; the owner had to contend with the hazards of hostile Aborigines, snakes, spiders, isolation and intense heat with drought one moment, followed by floods the next.

There was the back-breaking work of clearing gum trees which were even tougher to chop than elms. The expense and effort of ridding the land of the blacks and the trees — even if trees were ring-barked — was enormous.

Nearly twenty years before Thomas Oxnam arrived Queensland had become a separate colony. In 1859 the government had almost given land away in an attempt to populate the new state. Men, bulls and sheep pushed north and west into the acres often too dry or isolated to support them.

The main stipulation for purchasers of crown property was permanent residence on the area allotted to avoid the evils of absentee landlords. Unlike Europe, the soil of Australia was not to be monopolized by a particular class — no hereditary aristocracy, no feudal system blocked the common man from possessing what he tilled. The only barriers to overcoming the old order were squatters, unrecognized claims by Aborigines who had hunted there for 30,000 years, and proof of money to stock and run the land. Although a homestead could be raided by black men with nullah-nullahs and boomerangs, it was protected by legislation from claims for debt, an incentive for men such.as Thomas Oxnam.

The drought broke that November at the beginning of the hot season when Mary started her small private school for a dozen girls. It was then that affection for her new land came. The roots of some Australian grasses have the power to lie dormant during protracted droughts and to revive when the rains come. Overnight the dust bowls of plains and paddocks were green with sprouting grass.

Part Two

Chapter Nine

Cooktown, Queensland

They stood there waiting for the clocks to strike, the bells to ring, waiting for the New Year, waiting for the New Decade, waiting for the 1880s. The Union Jack, faded by the fierce tropical sun and weathered by monsoons, hung limp from the flagpole; the brass trumpets and drums of the Fire Brigade Band thundered out 'God Save our Gracious Queen... God Save the Queen...' and 'Hurrah for the red, white and blue!' The O'Riley's, the O'Flannagans and the Maguires, though, would have rather saluted the Pope than give three hearty cheers for Queen Victoria. But a few minutes after midnight the mood of mateship pulled together these diverse people who had come to this new land of space and sunshine and hope. This year, this decade, was going to be better. Everything would be all right in this outpost in the white man's tropics; everyone was going to make it in the 1880s. Prospects had never seemed brighter; a general air of confidence reigned among the revellers that night. One shop boasted the banner: 'Peace, Power, Prosperity — God Save the Queen'. It had been put up by John Lequire Adams who owned the chemist shop — he was very Empire minded. With a big white beard, white suit and a pith helmet he liked to lead parades.

Lured by dreams, or driven by creditors, thousands of settlers who had migrated from Britain to Australian colonies in the 1860s and 1870s went North of the Tropic of Capricorn when Queensland gold-fever broke out. Shopkeepers sold businesses, lawyers flung down files, doctors galloped away from patients. The chance of gold induced men to overcome the dangers and hardships of living in far-away and inaccessible wilds. When gold was discovered at the Palmer River, the richest alluvial field found in the colony, Cooktown, seventy-five miles away, had sprung up out of the scrub at the mouth of the Endeavour River. The river had been named by Captain Cook during his seven weeks there in 1770 when repairing his ship, the *Endeavour*. Over a hundred years later the town was named after Cook.

The Queensland coast had few navigable ports and harbours so the river mouth was the nearest place for diggers to sell gold, spend money and hail a steamboat for a journey back to the world. From a calico and canvas settlement in 1873 it grew almost overnight into a thriving seaport. It was a last frontier town. Even Brisbane was separated by a thousand miles of gum trees. In Cooktown a European was twice remote: cut off from the older, well-established southern states of Australia, and distant from the civilized countries of which they were offshoots.

People travelled to Cooktown by boat, foot, horse or bullock waggon over a trail blazed through the bush. Charlotte Street, Cooktown, was a stirring sight when the packers and bullock drovers were loading up for the Palmer Goldfields. Bullock teams which took goods and people were run by four carriers, Wallace Brothers (Charley and Sandy), Jim Earle, Tom Morris and Reynolds Brothers. A great deal of transport was done by packers — some used horses, some horses and mules, and some just mules. The mule was the main vehicle of the rough by-ways. The crack packer outfit belonged to Ned Finn, 'The Flying Packer', a wiry, small Irishman famed for his safe deliveries and quick service. He got £100 per ton to the goldfields. But as the tracks became roads prices got lower. The amount a well-packed mule could carry was staggering — up to

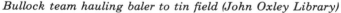

Bullock team hauling baler to tin field (John Oxley Library)

300 pounds. It seemed that the Chinese basket-carriers were competing with the mules — the tracks were lined with files of these wispy, barefoot coolies. Scores of the wretches, unable to stand the pace, their packs, the heat or the flies, dropped by the wayside. Some managed to get back to Cooktown with a queer form of paralysis of the legs. The leg trouble of these human beasts of burden was caused by the strain of the loads they carried — sometimes up to 200 pounds in two baskets attached to the ends of a pole slung across the shoulders.

In the first six years of traffic between Cooktown and the Palmer goldfields at least seventeen whites and Chinese were killed by Aborigines — a further ten were badly wounded and a further five rumoured dead.

The casualties of the carriers were higher. Spears killed 133 horses and 67 bullocks during those first six years, but the toll was probably greater.

The *Cooktown Courier* expressed the sentiments of some Cooktowners:

> When...a hardworking man loses at one fell swoop 10 or 11 horses of the average value of £40 or £50 he cannot be so very much to blame if he commits an indiscriminate act of slaughter amongst the blacks should he fall in with them...

The first year it was established an estimated 30,000 Europeans and Chinese passed through Cooktown and challenged the hazards of the tracks and the blacks to the *River of Gold*. And after a stint of prospecting they trudged back.

Tough living and careless spending meant prosperity in Cooktown; tents were replaced by weatherboard, zinc and corrugated iron structures. Granite from hills was used to build a few grand houses, gutters and drains to take the gush of monsoonal rains. It was a town of contrasts. The mimicry of Greek architecture — classical columns and ornate capitals added to shops to give permanence — looked incongruous beside weatherboard stores with gaudy signs and squat public houses.

Roads were made; forests cleared; bridges built; piers, jetties and lighthouses constructed; land was fenced in, planted, stocked and cultivated; churches, chapels and even a schoolhouse were established. Stone was quarried and by sheer muscle, spade, axe and mortar, civilized man changed the wilderness; changed what always had been.

Darwin's theory of evolution, during the twenty years since its publication, had been applied to many things, but not to Cooktown where everything was ephemeral, created today and, perhaps, gone tomorrow. Everyone in Cooktown came from somewhere else. Everyone was new. The town's society of English, Irish, Scottish,

Sail and tent makers (John Oxley Library)

German, Italian, Chinese and a few French, was not cohesive. Cooktown, like other towns in Australia, was a community of small groups, the unity of each coterie governed by religion, nationality, social class, money, manners or colour. The newly arrived would try to integrate, but couldn't — nothing had been established long enough to withstand additions. Of course, they reminded themselves, life here was better than in that forsaken place in Europe. Every man was establishing himself, 'on the make', comparing progress 'with the other bloke', looking over his shoulder. Each was a little distrustful and envious of the other. Grab or die; none of your moral code of the British Christian gentleman. Despite disparity among these men, aspirations were similar: quick money. Gold.

On Saturday nights at the West Coast the bush band with the good old piano accordion, mouth organ and melodious tin instruments beat it out; yarns were spun until at dawn they'd wind up with 'Rollin' home in the morning boys' or 'Pack up y're troubles in your old kit bag'.

Any man, yellow or white, coming in from a monotonous stint of dry work in the bush or the Palmer goldfields, was ready for riotous relaxation. To take away the feeling of self-exile, toasts were proposed in local rum, songs were vociferously sung. Many a night was spent chanting the Old Palmer Song:

I hear the blacks are troublesome,
And spear both horse and man,
The rivers are all wide and deep,
No bridges them do span,
No bridges them do span, my boys,
And you'll have to swim,
But never fear the yarns you hear,
And gold you're sure to win...

Cooktown was for the battler, the bloke from the bush with his back bent both from humping his swag and leaning on bar counters; his eyes blinking from corks hanging round a hat to keep the damn flies away. Oh for 'good tucker', fresh tobacco, debauchery, vice — and a bath. In the bush a man slept in his clothes and gave himself a shake when he woke up in the morning. He only saw his face in the back of a sardine tin. So no cake of Pears Soap was ever more welcome than in Cooktown. And no steak and kidney pie served with mashed potato ever tasted as it did there. After a bush diet of salt beef, roast kangaroo eaten out of a frying pan with a pocket-knife, or that frightful possum which had a strong gum-leaf flavour, a longing came for 'a proper meal'. Men went for weeks with nothing to sweeten their damper except an egg snatched from a wild bird's nest, or grubs, ants and boiled grass. Water was either excessive when summer monsoons made streams overflow, or non-existent. When rains failed, drought struck.

Food and self-interest were the same — failure meant starvation. Struggle often came down to 'tucker' and water, with a noggin' of rum to tune down the pain — until nuggets were found. Or something else.

That December night when Cooktowners waited for the glorious New Year, the Palmer River, undergoing the usual process of exhaustion, had yielded less gold — only a third of the total of previous annual totals. A lot of men, skint, had moved on. Although only six and a half years old, Cooktown was past its peak. But men still came to 'eat, drink and play'. Even the ugliest old hag thought she was a treasure; men outnumbered women by about four to one. In the 1876 census in North Queensland there were 21,907 males but only 5,582 females.

Cooktown still had over twenty establishments with drinking licences, as well as illicit grog shops which sold rum and water laced with laudanum. Countless bawdy houses did anything. The bruising of black eyes from drunken brawls was removed with live leeches kept in bottles on chemist shop counters. The 'damned yellow fella', otherwise known as John Chinaman, kept opium dens, cafes with aromas of incense and Oriental cuisine; gambling shanties playing Fan Tan, Gee Fah and Pak-a-Pu Banks; and joss houses with banging gongs and tinkling instruments, as well as brothels which soothed both yellow and white clientele. 'Turning this place into a New Canton', the whites would grumble. The Chinese inhabited houses and hovels of corrugated iron and wood. Coolies with their barefeet, pigtails and ambition, used to the subsistence conditions in China, could be content with less than the whites. The whites hated them: 'Go back to China, back to your sampans, Chin-Chin no belongee here'. In Cooktown, John Chinaman formed half the population of 5000, a number that swelled and dropped with arrivals and departures.

But now, on the last day of 1879, the heydays were really over, although few who stayed would admit it. Ships from all over the world laden with freights of flour, rice, mail, cotton, paint and eighteen-gallon kegs of whisky for the Scots, came with fewer opportunist diggers and settlers. And ships that departed had less gold bullion, but more stray emigrants, more sea-shell, tin, cedar, sandal-

*Chinese landing at Cooktown (*Illustrated Australian News *1874-5, National Library of Australia)*

92

wood and dried fish. Some men, though, got stuck in Cooktown. Returning from the Palmer River fields they found a job to earn the fare out, their escape, but somehow never moved on. Their jobs needed them. Debts, marriage, commitments — all became new roots. Some over-mortgaged properties in Charlotte Street had For Sale notices on them, others waited for a rise in values. Many buildings, so grand with notched cornices, run up in the good times, were now half tenanted. Some houses had even been taken down and shipped away to be erected in another town. Houses built of wood with narrow verandahs were dismantled as quickly as they had been put up.

As they stood there that last night of 1879, waiting for the new decade, waiting for the New Year, Captain Robert Watson felt for Mary's white-gloved hand. His grasp told her what he could not express in words. He loved her.

In the two and a half years since Mary had arrived in Queensland she had achieved the independence she had craved for so long, but now she was ready to forsake anything for this gentleman with horny hands. He had such a hold upon her heart. She could not control it; he blurred his way into whatever she was thinking, even though she did not know him well. How Papa would yell and go on if he knew! Captain Watson was the same age as Papa, forty-two, a Roman Catholic and a Scot. 'You'll meet Scotchmen wherever you go', Papa had joked. 'Just call out "Hey, Mac!" and you'll get a reply in broad Scots and a Mac will appear.'

And then he would add, 'And a damn Popish Mac at that! Since the Reformation the Roman Catholic Church and the English have grown apart — the differences are too great for marriage.'

But she hadn't seen dear, funny Papa for a year. She was still cross with him. He had tried to dissuade her from leaving the family, going independent, but he couldn't stop her. Papa had taken the family to Rockhampton for another fresh start after he had resigned from the Boiling Down Works saying, 'Damn those people wanting meat cubes! They're better off boiling old leather boots in the soup!' It had been an unhappy time; Mamma had had the joy of sending cards to Newlyn telling of the birth that year of the eleventh child, but two months later when the baby died black-edged letters followed telling of bereavement.

Nellie was getting married which left only the three boys and Carrie for Papa to support. Now that Mamma and Papa ran the Red Lion pub in Rockhampton they wouldn't have much time to spend with the children.

Mary had gone first to Brisbane where she had applied for a job in Cooktown advertised in the *Courier*. Monsieur Bouel had come expressly to the city, travelled the thousand miles south, to find 'a suitable governess for the two children'. The post had turned out not at all what she had expected and, like so many inhabitants of

93

Great Northern Commercial Family Hotel, Cooktown

Cooktown, Mary had thought of leaving, going south again, even made departure plans, but she was still there.

At last the bells rang out. It was midnight; it was 1880. As they sang Auld Lang Syne they knew it really was going to be all right now. They smiled and laughed and ignored the importuning of the Good Templars on a nearby box who were preaching against the two Australian vices: gambling and drink. It was time for champagne, for revelry; not time for lectures on 'The Evil of Drink', 'The Bible over the Bottle', and the 'Joys of Temperance'. Mary wanted to rush over and blurt, 'My father's a publican!' Silly people.

It was the best night Mary had ever had. 'No, I can't go home', she jokingly told Captain Watson. 'In Cornwall it's unlucky if a woman is the first to enter a house on the first day of the year. Good luck depends on a man taking the New Year in. If I go back do I know if a man has been before me?' As she said it she kept her eyes on his to convey that she did not believe the superstition.

Before dawn she and Captain Watson walked the 530 feet to the top of Grassy Hill — called Janellganell by the Aborigines — so she could see the sun rise.

'Australia's a nocturnal country', Captain Watson commented. 'Everything looks better at night. You don't notice the dryness or the space, the kangaroos, possums and koalas who often sleep through the hot days and come out at night.'

He held her hand tightly as he whispered, 'You never use my name! Why don't you call me Bob or Robert like most friends?'

Mary bit her lip, looked at the ground and then up to him. How could she say that she thought of him as 'Captain Watson' because he was older than her, like her father's circle?

'All right', she agreed, adding slowly, 'B-o-b!'

Captain Watson pushed an imaginary lock of hair across Mary's forehead so gently that his rough hands hardly touched her skin. He looked at her face. Their terrible loneliness had gone, now it was 'two hearts beating each to each...'

Breathless with the exertion of the steep climb to the top of Grassy Hill, Captain Watson and Mary lost their self-consciousness and the barriers which blocked so much in their lives disappeared. The trouble was that he was always too busy working to relax much with her, let alone amble along on walks.

'You must never go out in Australia without a stick and a hat', he lectured. They stared at the water far below as red hues of dawn fused into bright daylight. Mary could see the coral atolls and islands of the Great Barrier Reef which stretches for over a thousand miles parallel with the Queensland coast. 'Listen!' he continued. 'The stick's for the snakes and the hat's for the sun.'

Captain Watson's fishing depot, Lizard Island, was so far north that even in the bright light of that hot morning it could not be seen. To the east all was sea and islands; to the west trees. It was bewildering to think of the limitless square miles beyond, all covered with gum tree after gum tree, as far as Mary could see; her eye never came to the end of them.

'When Captain Cook came up here — 110 years ago — to spy his route out of the Great Barrier Reef, he was horrified. Look, you can see what he saw', explained Bob. 'The sea is criss-crossed with endless reefs. After six days sailing he stopped at my island, which he called Lizard Island because of all the four-legged reptiles there. He climbed the highest hill and there he found a clue to the labyrinth. Finally he got through into the open sea, just near where I live.'

Mary and Bob heard the maniac laugh of the kookaburra; they had the feeling of standing on the edge of the universe, beyond sundown.

A quiet strong man from the sea, Captain Watson was an acceptably safe father-figure. Like Mary he was an enterprising, hardworking, 'no nonsense' person and had little time for the froth of Cooktown. He came to the port, though, from time to time to sell catches of *bêche-de-mer* — the trepang, brown sea-slug or sea cucumber — so prized as a culinary delicacy by the Chinese in soups or braised with vegetables. Sometimes also referred to as sea ginseng, it was valued as a stimulant and aphrodisiac. Captain Watson and his partner, Percy Fuller, ran two boats crewed by Chinese and kanakas and were doing well. Captain Watson fished hard, not only because he was ambitious but because work was a substitute for contact with people; it gave him satisfactions and security that closeness with a woman, regular meals and substantial domestic comfort might have. Captain Watson and his brother, another sea captain, had come from Aberdeen two years before Mary had left England.

Short with reddish-fair hair, blonded from years of salt-air and sun, he had been doomed to perpetual courtship because always his income was inadequate for respectable middle-class marriage; his was a life of toil so as to shut out emotion.

It was later, when looking furtively at rosary beads in his camphor-wood box, that Mary saw some letters (rough first drafts which Bob had obviously copied in a better hand) to his sister in Edinburgh, that Mary understood more. When Bob first arrived in Queensland he worked on a station in the Darling Downs:

> ...I have not written to you for some time. The way I have been I was not inclined to write at all. Out of the eight weeks I was at Charon Station I was down five with the fever. The fever had never been so bad before. The two men died. Others went down to Brisbane, wrecks. It tore me about, no proper treatment. They used to give me a lot of quinine. Nothing to eat. I never ate any meat for a month. There was no one to wait on you, they were away at work all day. I shall never forget laying on that hard bed all day. I am still liable to get relapses at anytime. It has left me thin, hollow cheeked and weak. I won't be able to do any hard work...

Captain Watson had left school when he was twelve. He had told Mary, 'I always remember standing in the yard and the priest coming over. I knew it before he said it. "Your mother hasn't paid the fees. You will have to leave." ' His lack of formal education showed in his writing.

And another letter to the same sister:

> I was just thinking today how long it is since I seen you. It is four years and it will be five if you count this year. This part is an awful country. Fever stricken. There were twenty-five of our men down with it and my how those men suffered. Big strong men wasted away to shadows...

The letters got more cheerful when Captain Watson went to try his luck in Brisbane.

> I am going to a dance next week, evening dress affair. I am borrowing the coat and vest and hiring the pants. It is amusing but a person, more or less, feels a fraud; however, what the odds.
>
> Marry I cannot possibly think of it, and no one would like to more than me, suffering it is not to be, as I would sooner blow my brains out than marry and go on struggling more than before. I have had very little out of life and certainly will not get over much, once youth is gone. I look well over forty now, my hair is thinning, but what is the use of grumbling, a man has to take what comes with a smile. It seems that Mother is just the same as ever. She has no more willpower and insists on the rough time she has had. One thing, Betty, promise me do not be cross with her as it will make it worse. I never 'write cross' to her. Yes, I could have managed comfortably had things been normal and Mother an ordinary woman...

A further letter made Mary laugh:

I have developed into a wonderful dancer, went to third rate affairs to learn and kept at it. Do believe I have grown better looking but the thinning of my hair might rob me of that asset...Yes debt is a horrible thing, however, considering everything I am not tangled very much in that direction, a few pounds board, and my club dues...Note you are sending me some shirts, many thanks, but Alex must think me an awful humbug, he having a lean time and sending me clothes of his, however, no doubt some of the things are not much use to him, that suit for instance, with the worn seat, I had that fixed up and will get quite a good deal of service.

For a while Captain Watson tried to make a go of it away from the sea. He was determined he'd call no man his master, and like his father in Aberdeen became a commercial traveller.

A friend of mine who is in the importing business in a small way, is getting new samples out and I have been travelling for him, doing the wholesale trade for the past month, writing a little business, and getting a connection, that will, I hope, lead to a fair job, as it takes a fair while to get in with the market here in Brisbane for indents. One line, 'cheap pencils' I started on and never sold one for a week, however, I kept going, and got my first order 500 gross, from one man, and have sold over 2,000 gross, and when stocks of various houses run low I will get their orders. I have taken orders for torch cases, electrical goods, bamboo racks etc... I don't know if my friend will be able to advance my commission on all sales, however, to date he has. He is a very decent chap and teaching me the inside of the importing business, in fact, we go for a swim every Sunday together...I have prospects of getting on.

Chapter Ten

French Charley's

It had been a very hot airless day at the start. The summer in North Queensland is too hot to be pleasant. The thermometer had read more than 100 degrees in the coolest part of the house; the butter had melted into thin oil and the milk had turned sour. Everything had seemed too hot to touch. Mary was wearing the lightest of stays but she was still uncomfortable. The tropical climate of the north coast was considered deadly for white men — assumed to be a country where the white man would wither and the black man would thrive. The stifling damp heat Mary could somehow bear but the insects! Oh the itch.

On that last meeting before Captain Watson had sailed away in his lugger to Lizard Island he had said, 'See you Friday'. All day at the house Mary had jumped everytime the gate in the white picket fence swung and banged or a footstep sounded on the verandah. She even jumped at the rattle of cart wheels clattering as they swung around the corner of Hope and Walker Streets. By 5 o'clock when she strolled down Charlotte Street to French Charley's where she played the piano every evening she concluded that he had meant Friday night. Would he risk sailing into the harbour in the dark? Was he shipwrecked on one of the reefs? *Bêche-de-mer* fishermen had terrible accidents; sea wasps and stone fish injected toxins into victims and dispensed instant death. Sharks with long sinister fins and hundreds of teeth were voracious.

Mary drew her shoulder blades together and revolved the top of her arms so that the starched lace on her chemise would achieve what her hands could not. She longed to scratch the detestable bites, but desisted even though the irritation from mosquitoes, sandflies, fleas or whatever unknown crawling tropical mite had buried its proboscis in her flesh, was stinging. The chemise, alas,

98

Charlotte Street, Cooktown

was ineffective. 'Those jolly Chinese', thought Mary. 'They've
dipped the clothes in boiled rice water instead of using starch.
Darn!' Not able to bear the itch a moment longer, slowly she lifted
her fingers above the keyboard of the pianoforte and raised her right
hand until it was behind the lace collar of her navy blue poplin frock.
Miss Moore's voice echoing from the past stilled her. 'A young lady
never scratches or rubs herself. She never uses fingernails — not for
anything. Restraint, girls!' Dear Miss Moore with severe blue eyes,
skin of ancient ivory and that erect head always held six inches
higher than the person she addressed. Dignity, control and a Christian consideration for others was what she stood for. By 'Christian'
Miss Moore meant 'protestant' — like Queen Victoria she was
intensely hostile to the catholic religion.

The restaurant was filling up, but Captain Watson still hadn't
arrived. As the room got hotter Mary could feel more bites swell on
her skin. They must be sandfly bites, hot air always brings up the
lumps, she thought. The restaurant kitchen had a tame carpet-bag

snake which Monsieur Bouel had trained to catch rats, and a few geckoes to devour insects, but it was little defence. Again Mary leaned back to rub her spine on the curve of the bentwood chair, but Miss Moore's voice prevented her scratching. How Miss Moore would gasp if she knew that Mary was 'entertaining at the pianoforte' at French Charley's — a flashy place with too many mirrors, too much gilt and too many yards of cheap velvets. 'The quintessence of vulgarity!' would have been her comment.

Mary wrote regularly to her former head-mistress but her letters omitted the fact that in remote Cooktown duties as children's governess extended to being pianist at her employer's restaurant. It would have been difficult to explain that Monsieur Bouel was a rogue, but she liked him.

Although it took only five months now before Mary received replies to any comments — the P & O mail steam boats to England were getting swifter — by the time they came, the issues had changed and the remarks seemed irrelevant. Miss Moore's letters, mostly about school and tidings of former schoolfellows, were sent in bulky envelopes full of cuttings from the *Royal Cornwall Gazette* on anything connected with Newlyn. She might as well have sent news about the moon. It all seemed so remote and far away. Distance was emphasized by the fact that Mary, like many emigrants who had not found gold or luck, was stuck in Cooktown. With neither the fare to go south nor the courage or energy to tackle yet another fresh start she stayed, modestly striving to do her duty. England, was it 12,000 or 16,000 miles? A distance beyond concept; it had to be calculated in days not miles. So she played on at French Charley's and taught Bouel's children part-time.

Mary's well-trained fingers danced up and down the ivory keyboard, her right foot pumping the pedal. Oh, she was so happy being a pianist, earning her living at what she liked best in the world. Her head and body swayed in rhythm with the tune. It did not matter about all those other problems. Faster, faster... the beat was so good.

Mary kept glancing sideways towards the arched side doorway that opened onto the side street to encourage both the breeze and customers. She was cross that her attention was fixed on Captain Watson. Why, she thought, is feeling beyond control and definition? Where was Captain Watson? The main doorway was opposite the Adelaide Steamship and Navigation Company Wharf, better known as the ASN wharf, and as a ship had just tied up the door was closed so that no riff-raff would wander in. Mary often heard Monsieur Bouel remark that the ASN ran a flotilla of villainous boats with no regard to the comfort and convenience of passengers. He loathed anything to do with ASN ships, their wharf or men.

A constant dispute raged about his rights to be where he was. In 1873, before the government surveys, Bouel had built a restaurant on land set aside officially for wharf-side facilities. He was later

Charlotte Street, Cooktown (John Oxley Library)

ordered to quit, but appealed, saying his business was entirely for the convenience of sea-farers. He had, he declared, expended £1,000 or more on fitting out the restaurant. The appeal, which went to Brisbane, was dismissed. Told to move, he went a little further up the road, but still behind the main wharves in the premier position on the south side of Charlotte Street, the first place after the wharves.

A clever Frenchman, a wonderful charlatan, Bouel had a kind heart but was mixed up in many a shady scheme. He was also much of a dreamer. He wanted to start a sugar industry in New Guinea using the local natives as labour, although the country was still regarded as no man's land. Another of his schemes involved the establishment of a *Mont de Piété*, so that the temporarily embarassed might finance themselves in modest undertakings at a small rate of interest.

To give his restaurant an atmosphere appropriate to its name he had waitresses coached in French — but customers who crossed them found their command of English invective very powerful! Nevertheless, it was the smartest place in Cooktown. Bouel, a fine host, had the tastiest food in the North, the prettiest girls and the best bar.

101

When regular customers saw their reflections in the bevelled mirrors behind the bar they thought they were somewhere exclusive, somewhere 'with class'. Really, though, it was all rather tawdry. Captain Watson had been horrified when told that Mary was the pianist there; absolutely shocked. He had heard that cabaret girls wore eleven petticoats and were thrown nuggets by miners to remove layers progressively.

Mary looked sideways again. Through the arched doorway she saw the lamp-lighter moving along briskly, flaming the posts with a stick. Tonight he was late; he usually came before sunset for night falls quickly in the tropics. Oh, where was Captain Watson?

Mary was temporarily diverted from anxiety by her irritating mosquito bites. 'I will get some methylated spirits and dab it on', she decided, although it meant going out to the backyard and half undressing in the lavatory. Refinements such as 'indoor conveniences' were impossible as Cooktown had no proper sewerage.

The waitresses at French Charley's changed and repainted their complexions in a room on the left of the kitchen. But Mary avoided both the room and those hussies with their low-cut silks, satins and make-up — pink rouge, thick black mascara, blue eye-shadow, scarlet lipstick and cream powder applied thickly so it would not melt even when the thermometer climbed to over 102 degrees. These soft and silly women who ignored the rigidity of British codes governing sexual behaviour and slept with men for money and gain, made Mary conscious that she was the product of an irregular union. She held her head higher than usual.

She now called herself Mary Phillips-Oxenham in anticipation of the day that she would show her birth certificate. While she was at it she added the name Beatrice — it had been mean of Papa to have her christened so late and to give her only one name.

Just as Mary was about to rise from the piano to go outside she felt a presence behind her. Captain Watson? No, it was Hans Müller, a Bavarian swelling with beef and beer and importance. A Lutheran, he had migrated from Hanover when in his teens, a good thirty years ago. He was hearty, paunchy and sentimental — a digger and a capitalist who employed another digger to stand knee deep in the Palmer River to do the back-breaking work of sifting gold in pannikins. When Hans went to the gold fields he carried more sieves than the Queen's cook had in her kitchen; he would try anything to get more precious metal from the wet dirt and stones. For Mary it was the same old story, although in Newlyn the search had been for silver. She had gone from silver to gold. Miners at home in Cornwall were mostly tributers — the silver miner only took a percentage of what was gained from the earth. They were down-trodden compared to these carefree men. An opportunist Australian miner sold his gold and, elated by coins in his pockets and notes in his jacket, went on a spree and frittered away his winnings.

Hans, different from other miners, had invested gold profits in

Cooktown by buying a bakery on the hill. His lack of popularity was caused by his refusal to surrender the umlaut over his name painted on the bakery window. It remained MÜLLER with two dots over the U despite the Cooktown pressure, especially from those who had floated up to being the leaders of the new community, men who had 'got on', to conform to English spelling. The English had an ingrained superiority to other nations — now peppered with racialist infusions of Darwinism and theories about inferior races and the survival of both the fittest and the best.

Mr Müller, who considered himself a gentleman, dumped his large body into a varnished bentwood chair near Mary. 'The *Corea's* come in', he drawled in an attempt to interrupt the piano recital. But Mary kept her hands on the piano as he droned on, turning her head and smiling occasionally, waiting for a pause to ask a question, something she had been pondering. What Mary played did not matter, the music was to fill the room, to close gaps in banal conversations, to block out the night shrill with cicadas and croaking frogs.

Away from the blackboard, chalk and safety of being queen of the schoolroom, Mary, with an active self-determinate drive, tended to make difficulties — even if they did not exist — just for the pleasure of demonstrating her influence and her ability to put matters in order. This desire to be in command and to organize things as she thought right, had an effect on her relationships, with women and men alike. Mary, convinced of her own worth, knew she had a

The Palmer coach leaving Cooktown

definite place in the scheme of things, but she was unwilling to accept that it was an insignificant one. Nor was she prepared to agree that her role should be passive, for she did not acknowledge that because she was a woman she was an emotionally weak, inferior being. She tended to be intolerant of women who appeared to lack her strength of will, and resented men who wanted to dominate her. Contemptuous of many customers — miners, sea captains with sunburnt faces, would-be's in suits tailored on credit — Mary was aloof. She would have looked prettier if she hadn't parted her dark hair in the middle and tugged it back severely. A few curls might have softened that stubborness in her jaw.

Mary kept her hands on the piano as Mr Müller droned on. Finally she stopped and said, 'I have noticed that the Australian crow doesn't make the "caw" sound of the English rook, but that they call out in harsh tones, the German word "Ach". What does it mean?'

Before he had time to answer a tarty barmaid who called herself by the unlikely name of Nicole came up with a hearty hello for Mr Müller. She considered Mary 'stuck-up like'.

Mary's self-made navy blue poplin frock with a lace Peter Pan collar contrasted the bare-shouldered Nicole in silk and satin whose appearance showed she would sing loud and lift petticoats high to kick the can-can.

'Untrained mind and overdressed body', Mary said to herself. She would go and dab methylated spirits on the bites now, she decided, glancing at the doorway for Captain Watson. As she crossed the floor she heard Nicole, 'Just b'coz she's been to boardin' school and had heducation she thinks she's lady muck. But I tell ya with me beauty and figger I ain't agoing to take 'er any longa. She shall be 'orf.'

At last methylated spirits stung the bites. The relief! Walking back to the kitchen, Mary found an empty champagne bottle and filled it with Moselle and beer, gave it to her friend, John, the wine waiter, and returned to the piano. He approached the table at which Mr Müller and Nicole were sitting.

'The complements of the establishment', said the wine waiter, placing the bottle which was now standing in a silvered bucket full of crushed ice from the new ether-evaporating iceworks. Mary watched incredulously; neither noticed their ghastly drink as they ordered a late supper. The girls chose from menus after reading from right to left, finding the most expensive item and ordering it.

As Mary attempted to scratch above her ankle with the point of her other shoe, she tumbled from the chair and crashed to the floor. Captain Watson was helping her up.

'How on earth did you lose your balance in the middle of Strauss?' he questioned and laughed when he heard.

She noticed he was wearing new clothes. Months later she discovered that his late arrival was caused by the distraction of the

104

gambling table at the Sea Wah hotel. But then he often did things, not because of a desire, but to assert himself against Mary. Few people, few men at forty-two, were as thrillingly unencumbered as Captain Watson. He had no responsibility or commitment. Not one person — neither family, employer nor child — relied on him. No home to keep. He should have been the lightest and happiest of men, being able to wake up and know there was nothing he *had* to do. He was free! Why does any man give up an easy and reckless life? No job. No boss. No children. No wife. No real home. But he saw little joy in his freedom. A deep loneliness cut into him that he thought marriage would cure. When men were lonely they stooped to any companionship: dog, horse or woman became comrades or friends. Woman or animal were showered with caresses and conversations, not because of who they were but because of their availability. And in a new place like Cooktown people talked so much twaddle. Men lose something vital when they uproot themselves from their native environment.

Oh, how he, Captain Watson, found comfort in the shabby, genteel plain strong girl, down at heel and so uncertain of her background and status.

Chapter Eleven

Marriage

It had all been rather vexing. In the end she had just added a year to her age, so that she did not have to get parental permission. What a fuss Papa had made. 'A man my age?' he had roared. 'A mixed marriage never works either. Going to bow your head to female idols, eh?' It was so complicated — her being illegitimate and not wanting Bob to find out — and if she did admit to her correct age he might ask why the letter of authority was from Mamma and not Papa.

And then Bob had wanted her to change religion; tried to turn her, he had. When she had gone back to Rockhampton to get her trousseau and say goodbye, Mamma had said, 'Dear, are you sure, is it quite safe for you to go to such a place? Lizard Island?'

It was only when her parents had seen her Moroccan leather travelling case with the initials rubbed out and re-engraved as M.W. that they sighed and agreed to Mary marrying Captain Watson.

Carrie, who was then twelve years old, was to go with her. The purpose of this decision was blurred. Mary thought it was to give Mamma and Papa a rest. Mamma thought it was for company for Mary on the island.

The only thing there was plenty of was trees for firewood. Fire was free. But water was nearly always scarce so marriage meant not only sharing the bed, but sharing the bathwater which had to be carried in buckets and boiled on wood that first had to be chopped. It was different, of course, when the monsoon came. Usually much could be deduced from a relationship in the outback or bush towns by observing who — the husband or the wife — got into the bath-tub first. Cleanliness was exhausting. And revealing.

Captain Watson and Mary were married on 30 May 1880 at Christ Church in Furneaux Street. What Mary had missed most at the ceremony had been sweet church bells pealing joyously from a tower. Such a funny little weatherboard church, like a large new shed. But at least they were married there and not in the Catholic Church down the hill! Oh, what a horror that would have been: Latin and candles and bells. During the service the psalms and responses had been chanted by a mixed congregation of ladies and gentlemen, including a few friends from French Charley's.

The week's honeymoon had been a bit of a trial, but mostly good. They had thought of travelling south to a place near Bloomfield. However, the blacks were bad at the time so they stayed in Cooktown. In between Cooktown and the Palmer River spears flew fast and furious; hills echoed with the piercing ricochet of rifles, revolvers and shouts of 'The blacks, quick the blacks!' Many whites who ventured into the bush never returned; it was war to the knife. The Aborigine said a certain tract of land was his territory, it always had been. The white man said the Aborigines were trespassing. Even the 'tame mob' of blacks that came to town in grubby blankets said, 'That-me-country'. But intrepid savages, hunted from billabongs and places where forebears had found food and drinkable water, driven into barren ranges, shot like wild dogs, retaliated

Aborigines c.1886 (John Oxley Library)

Mounted police setting off on patrol, Cooktown (John Oxley Library)

when and how they could. Spears and boomerangs were hurled at cattle, horses and men and often killed them. These blacks, though never strictly head-hunters, when starving would let an odd European or Asian furnish a meal.

In the south only ritual cannibalism was practised — part of a dead person, a child or relative, was ingested to affirm affinity. Although there were exaggerated reports because of misinterpretation of such things as 'double burial' and the carrying around of bones of people greatly treasured, it was different around Cooktown in the north where whites were known to have been eaten.

Settlers, imbued with the idea of 'keeping the blacks out', just used guns — there is only one recorded case in North Queensland where a large group of natives were poisoned by damper laced with arsenic. The 'damn natives' were wild and hungry north of the Tropic of Capricorn, fiercer than the southern Aborigines. Over 20 per cent of the early white workforce in Queensland had been killed by the blacks: an estimated 350 to 400 whites were killed from the

108

1860s to the 1890s plus innumerable Chinese. Since the European and Chinese influx around Cooktown, a fitful war of extermination had been waged. Murder countered murder, outrage was repaid by violence, theft by robbery, shots by spears, vengeance by vengeance. Killing was bad enough, rape worse, but cannibalism made the blacks 'degraded wretches'. In some Aboriginal languages human flesh was *talgoro*; and white men were referred to by the same word as that used for evil spirits.

More and more land was claimed by whites as their own. After all, the government had sold it to them. The government! The heritage of myth and rites of tribes was threatened; supplies of edible birds and fish were diminishing. Some Aborigines left the tribes of their forefathers and sought an earthly paradise of rum, blankets and tobacco. Nearly every station had one or two black boys employed as stock-riders; they were invaluable for tracking lost sheep and cattle but they were not submissive enough to make good employees. And they were incurable nomads, going walkabout without any notice.

Chapter Twelve

Lizard Island

Four days after Captain Watson placed the gold ring on Mary's third finger he was ready to sail her seventy miles north to Lizard Island. Madame Bouel had warned after the ceremony, 'A wife just takes over where the mother leaves off', but the new Mrs Watson felt herself the happiest of women.

After breakfast, taking deep breaths and courage, Mary and Carrie clambered onto the *Isabella* on the long jetty north of the main wharf. Low tide meant they had to climb down a ricketty ladder. The boat resembled Noah's Ark for Mary had collected twenty hens, ten ducks, two pigs.

The voyage was made in ideal conditions: the sky was blue, there was sufficient wind to get them going fast, but not enough to cause too many waves, only ruffle the water which was a transparent blue. The scenery all down the coast of Queensland was very wild, and occasionally beautiful. Endless wooded mountain ranges of gum trees ran along the mainland down to beaches.

Bob carried a mass of detailed knowledge in his head about the vagaries of the tides, the dangers of the hidden reefs, the eddies and counter-currents caused by shoals and obstructions. 'The first sign of a coral atoll is the sea which breaks against it', Bob explained to Mary. The voyage brought back all the horrors of the *City of Agra*, of leaving Cornwall, of the alienation. The three years had stretched; it seemed longer ago than that.

He never had to tell her when they saw Lizard Island. She knew. It looked very beautiful in the early evening when the mountains were turning to that soft clear smoky blue, peculiar to Australian scenery. Beside the high peaked island straight ahead was a tiny hill in the water, Eagle Islet. As their boat got close to shore and turned

Aerial view of Lizard Island (Queensland Department of Tourism)

north, Mary could smell the pungent wood-smoke from the perpetual fire of mangrove bushes used for smoking the *bêche-de-mer*. Or could she? They were now in a small horseshoe-shaped inlet. Bob lit the kerosene lantern and said, 'Wait', and went ashore and got three stools which he placed in the low water for Carrie and Mary to walk on. His back was too bad to carry them.

Percy Fuller was there — all tall and affable and English — to welcome her. Some black boys, kanakas, lurked in the shadows. The two Chinamen didn't come out. Mary couldn't see much when they walked to the house, as it had become quite dark. Dried leaves rustled underfoot. She had a strange feeling that she was walking across a wilderness where human feet had never trod, although she knew she was wrong. There was Bob, Mr Fuller and those boys that helped with the fishing.

The dwelling, her home, was truly solid. Forty paces from the sandy beach, it was made from large granite stones cemented together; hardened earth was the floor, a thatch over corrugated iron was the roof. There were three rooms. Clothes hung up on five nails; a trunk was a table covered with playing cards, another trunk a seat; pictures from an old calendar were tacked on the wall above a mattress on the ground.

The top of a tobacco tin lay filled with cigarette stubbs. From the ceiling hung a knotted mosquito net. Some dinner-dishes, no, it was washing, was steeping in a basin in a far corner. Mary remembered Mrs Hosken in Newlyn. She laughed inside — everything is easier when it is warm. Bob was busy uncrating the hens and ducks. It was too late, the light was too dim, to unpack her possessions.

'Have you towels and a basin or something to wash in?' Mary asked her husband mischievously. 'A pitcher and soap? A pail for

111

water? A broom? A tea-pot? A little milk jug and sugar bowl?'

Somehow they washed; a Chinese boy appeared with food. Not a meal she or Carrie wanted to eat. But she was happy, there was a lovely feeling of quiet and of space; of being cut off. Here she was now living in the South Seas amongst the islands and coral reefs and tall fishing boats. Not a white settlement worthy of the name broke the solitude between Cooktown and Cape York, nothing hardly for 400 miles. Unlike the last months at Newlyn, the time at Maryborough, the tense existence at Cooktown, here she felt a link. A safety. Lizard Island was home. It was a wonderful clear night of stars.

What the honeymoon couple did not know was that they had chosen a sacred island, that within 200 yards of the house was an Aboringal bora ground. All Mary knew was that the place had a special feel about it, strange. In the white, hot sunlight, under the eucalyptus trees the next morning Mary saw that the long period of isolation had endowed Lizard Island with prehistoric forms of life. The Lizards: sometimes they moved; sometimes they stayed motionless on the rocks, almost like shrunken monsters or dinosaurs.

Before it got too hot Mary and her husband climbed the peak on the island. They threaded their way up over boulders, heaped up

rocks, logs and through the tufts of spinifex. Mary jumped. Coming slowly towards them, his arm propelling him, was a long dragon-like creature. At first she had not seen it for the four-foot long lizard with brown-green scales blended in with the rocks.

'Shush', whispered Bob, 'It's only a monitor, a good old goanna! Won't hurt you. Lizards are really harmless. Except they are a nuisance, they carry off the hens' eggs and are always after meat. Even if they bit you they wouldn't really cut deep because they only have a scaly jaw. Quick, look, his eyelid is moving.' The creature shot out his tongue to catch an insect, and then remained motionless, just staring.

Determined to get to the top Mary kept her moans to herself. From time to time they rested and viewed the miles of sea around them. The rough quartz in the granite boulders scratched Mary's hand as she levered herself up the steep rocks. At last they got to the crest of the 1,200 foot mountain and stood where Captain Cook had stood 110 years earlier. What a panorama!

To the east they saw the broken white lines of foaming waves, the surf breaking on the outer edge of the Great Barrier Reef. The line was endless, disappearing into the horizon at each end. Although from this height they could view, in the far distance, the green mountains of the Queensland coast, when they were below in their little homestead bay they could see nothing but the motionless expanse of blue Coral Sea. But now on the top of Mt Cook Mary did not feel so isolated from the world, so alone. Between the island and the mainland Mary saw three large reefs, white and rectangular at low tide. And joining the windy leeward side of the island, she saw little Eagle Islet.

'Nothing's changed', said Bob, 'It's been the same for centuries. Man has not yet changed what always has been.'

Mary, gripping onto a rock, for she felt giddy when she looked down, ventured, 'But there, down below, it's certainly different'.

Directly below Mt Cook, on the lowland, almost on the small, sandy bay beside the creek which ran into the sea, was the Watson house. Apart from the homestead area much of the island was rocky and barren — rugged land with large and small lumps of granite partially covered by long grass. Everywhere were stunted shrubs and boulders, jumbled together in picturesque confusion. It was the tropic winter so everything was dry, as it usually was from April till December.

At last they descended. Mary and Bob stood on a ridge near their bay. In the middle of the day Australian birds retire to the cool shade of shrubs and trees. Everything was quiet. Mary felt the accumulated silence of a million years around. As she lent on the boulder in a cool gully she felt that perhaps just here the sound of a human voice had never been heard before. When Bob spoke, though, the sensation of the lifeless solitude of the Australian bush vanished.

Chapter Thirteen

The World of an Island

From a distance above the lagoon the black sorcerer used fervour, all he possessed, as he directed the death-bone towards the brown cottage at the edge of the bay. The tribe reserved the bone for use against dreadful enemies. So potent is the magic spell of the death-bone that it causes unfathomable and awful mysteries.

When the Carandjie — chief medicine man — pointed the death-bone on Lizard Island that June day in 1880 towards Captain Watson and his bride, it was with vigorous hate. He wanted the white trespassers to go away, to leave the Bora ground; here every stone, every rock, every grain of earth and sand was sacred. Aborigines believed not only in the former existence of ancestors endowed with superior powers but also in other more superior beings. Some tribes believed that long ago in the Dreamtime there were two such beings called Ungambikula, meaning made out of nothing. They lived in the sky, came down and made men and women, and then turned into lizards.

This isolated island was for lizards — not for humans; not a spot to toil. It was assigned to ancestral beings and spirits which haunted the trees near the water-hole in the hollow. These arrogant white intruders were building shelters on the tribe's special land; land reserved for ceremonials directed by the moon, the sun and the stars.

Uninitiated boys or women were never brought over from the mainland to Lizard Island and now a white woman was living in the cottage. Chinamen with pigtails were disturbing the sacred earth by digging in it and growing more plants; worse though, they killed the lizards who ate the hens' eggs.

When Captain Cook had stayed overnight on the island 110 years earlier in August 1770 — after baffling attempts to sail between shoals, reefs and breakers — he saw great heaps of empty shells. He concluded that natives only visited this uninhabited granite outcrop for special feasts. It must, he wrote, have significance to tempt natives to venture the fifteen miles of treacherous sea from the mainland in flimsy dugout canoes. As he saw no animals except lizards, every sort from geckoes to large reptiles, he called this tropic paradise Lizard Island. Cook noted that the island, about ten miles in circumference with a few sandy bays, was barren except for a hollow of low land on the north-west side covered with long grass and trees.

One hundred and nine years had passed from the time of Captain Cook's departure to Captain Watson's arrival. Naked men with upper lips and chests streaked with white and red ochre, stared silently at Captain Watson, his partner, Percy Fuller, and their six employees, as they built the small fishing station in 1879. A few huts, the two-roomed cottage and the smoke-house established the firm 'Messrs Fuller & Watson, *Bêche-de-mer* Fishers & Suppliers, Lizard Island, via Cooktown'.

Occasionally the Scottish fisherman had fired snider rifles into the air when he heard wailings and didgeridoos in the distance, but there had been no serious trouble.

Everyone was armed. Lying in the long grass on the lowland at Lizard Island, Bob Watson taught his bride how to respond to an ambush with both snider rifle and pistol. She could soon hit a half-crown at seven yards. Many a merry afternoon was spent shooting coins along the smooth hard sand on the beach. Now, though, whenever natives were on the hills it wasn't just pistol practice, it was to 'let them hear it. Scare 'em, just in case.'

Bob's partner, the quiet Percy Fuller, had moved out of the cottage into a wooden one-roomed cabin near the smoke and boiler house, but he was usually away fishing or in Cooktown selling the catch so the Watsons were often alone on their island — a whole world it was — except for the two male Chinese servants, transient employees, a few kanakas and those 'damn black fellows' when they visited The Lizards. Occasionally Mr Green, one of Captain Watson's employees, came for a few days.

Carrie stayed exactly six months. Mary wrote in the front page of her 1881 diary:

Carrie returned to Rockhampton per *Wotonga* on 4th December, 1880. Mr. Fuller left for Melbourne per 11th December. Bob and self left Cook-town 2.30 p.m. December 11th for the Lizards. Mr. Green and Ah Ping aboard....Boats *Petrel* and *Isabella* went to Eagle Island December 16th. Mr. Green in charge of *Petrel*, Ah Ping in charge of *Isabella*...

The diary continued:

...French Man of War bound for New Guinea anchored in the bay about 3.30 pm. Friday Dec. 31st.

1st January. Saturday. Bob went to the Man of War. One Muscovy duck dead. Made a pair of pyjamas. Had a game of whist after tea. Mr. Green and dummy, self and Bob. Heavy rain. Good tide. Wind changeable.
2nd January. Sunday. Heavy rain all morning. Bob and Mr. Green stopping leaks about the house and store. Fine afternoon and evening. Wind variable.
3rd January. Monday. Fine day, sea rough. *Petrel* aground. Bob did some garring. Mr. Green making window shutters... Thunderstorm about 7 o'clock, fish not brought home... Bob and Mr. Green gone to make boats secure.
4th January. Tuesday. Washed out soiled clothes, dried and put them aside. Finished book *Lamplighter*. Fish brought around. Boys culling fish after dinner. Thunder, lightning and rain...
6th January. Thursday. Mr. Green brought *Petrel* from south side of the island, Ah Ping with *Isabella* called for a load of wood. Bob rafted two logs from south side. Black boys cutting wood after dinner. Bob after dinner acting cobbler to a pair of reef boots. Made bread, gingerbread cake a success. Fine day, moderate breeze. Wind S.E.

The diary entries in the front of the Lett's *Australasian Rough Diary* were written carefully, in the same way that Mary had made entries in the school log-book. At the back of the journal, though, hidden under 'Cash Account January', concealed in reports of her beloved poultry, she noted the unhappiness.

Saturday January 1st. Bob wanted to move the table farther into the middle of the room. I objected. Consequence a slight disturbance.
January 3rd. Chicken died. Two and a half hour's search for 2 young ducks. Found over near smoke house. Ducks died.
January 7th. Muscovy duck died.
January 12th. Eleven chickens all well. 4 Muscovy and 3 ducks do well. Bob discovered ducks' nest — eleven eggs in it, duck sitting. Already a week on Moses.
January 14th. Bob and Mr. Green a few hearty words over a log of wood and fishing off reefs.
January 17th. Chick killed.
January 18th. Discovered delicate chick dead this morning.
January 19th. Another chicken dead, think it had been trodden on.
January 20th. A slight fright by discovering Sambo standing by my bedroom door. He had been walking in his sleep, told me it was 'devil devil'.
January 25th. Bob slightly annoyed did not hear me answer him about putting an egg under a sitting hen. Both very silent.

February 2nd. Bob and self great row. Self half mad all about my not answering him when spoken to.
February 3rd. Recovered from the slight disturbance of yesterday, Bob still rubs his own back.
February 10th. Black young pullet hatched eight pullets. Six chickens and one of her own, only sat on one egg. One chick dead. Two nice rock melons from Bob's little garden.
February 17th. Chinese fishing boat from Cooktown yesterday fished on the S.E. side came around tonight.
February 18th. Bob and self made a bet of 5s that Mr Fuller was on his

116

way back self that he was not.

February 24th. Bob and self row again, all about the dead ducks. I did not make any answer when he said something about the weather.

February 25th. Both very silent.

February 26th. More chatty, nearly all right.

February 27th. Things as usual.

Cash A/c March

March 16th. Myself in the wars again about the bedroom floor.

March 17th. Both very silent ...I have need to speak of necessity — alas I would not have done... awful... with the *answer* Bob gave me when I called him to get up.

March 18th. Very miserable. Bob's opinion came out at tea; very small.

March 19th. Row over, things comfortable.

Mary was not an easy person to live with for she enjoyed an argument. A lot of the troubles with Bob were caused because although she accepted the prevailing concept of paternal authority in family life, and was ready to follow father or husband-led enterprise, she did not obey blindly, but questioned first so she could feel sure that all was right.

Despite her strong will and her associated refusal to accept easy defeat, Mary did have a softer side. Indeed, her capacity for showing affection was considerable — her resistance to male superiority was partly because of an instinctive fear. She knew she was vulnerable. Emotionally — for safety — she wished to keep men at arm's length.

Mary did not understand the Neanderthal-like men; embarrassed by their naked buttocks she was forced to turn her head the other way. Thank goodness they sometimes wore loin aprons of leaves, feathers or grass — they could not weave cloth. To observe one of the most primitive cultures of mankind was shattering to Mary; she shuddered when she recalled Bob's tales of their eating wasp-larvae, witchetty grubs, squashed ants, frogs and even poor Edward Boyd who'd been boomeranged and speared at Hell's Gate on the Palmer Track. But Mary herself felt no hostility to the Aborigines; they were too different and too much a part of everyday life. It seemed unfair to her that they were being suddenly invaded. During Captain Cook's seven weeks at the mouth of the Endeavour River there had not been any trouble with them except when they wanted one of Joseph Banks' turtles and angrily set fire to nearby grass when he refused to give them one.

Since his ancestors had first inhabited this dry continent the Aborigine had never had to contend with any higher race and had had no impetus given by competition with other people. Yet the indigenous culture was obviously able to adapt and accept outside influences. An Aboriginal cricket team had even toured England in

1868! And they learnt languages quickly — and well. In some ways the Aborigines were ingenious. Not only had they invented the boomerang with its peculiar twist which resisted normal forces, they also had a unique way of measuring a tree. They walked in a straight line away from the tree trunk until by bending down and looking between their legs they could see the very tip of the tree — the height of the tree was equal to the distance walked.

A desire to 'follow the fashion' sent most white women in Australia about in clothes of the chilly temperate zone of Europe. Fashion made little concession to climate but Mary did. Her camisole was seldom worn and although she still liked voluminous skirts she wore just one of her three petticoats. Only on smart occasions did she hook a small crinoline inside her skirt or lace her stays really tight. Mary kept up the lady-like role expected of the aspiring-middle-classes of England, even though its gracious ways were hardly adaptable to life on a tropical island.

A desire to follow fashion

An entry from Mary's diary describes a day of domestic calm, despite a thermometer recording of 100 degrees in the shade: 'Made bread and cakes. Gingerbread success. Wedding ring slipped off my finger. Found it later in the knife box when laying table. Made a flannel shirt for Bob, also two tablecloths. We had an early tea and spent a long evening outside humming a few songs and enjoying the moonlight.'

Even though Ah Sam was willing to help in the house he worked in the garden and in preparing the *bêche-de-mer*. Mary had seen Madame Bouel's Chinese cook stoning raisins for cakes with his teeth, moistening dough for pastry by spitting on it, and taking yeasted dough to bed to make it rise. Still, the Chinese were the only domestic workers available. Aborigines were not considered to be servile enough to make even bad servants. And they were unable to grasp some concepts. Bob had told Mary about the young Aboriginal girl on a large station who had kept her feet warm while milking by sitting with her feet in the bucket of fresh milk.

The Watson fish station was a bee-hive of productiveness, even a wooden shanty laundry was built. A few old weather-boards were roughly nailed together for a lean-to, roofed with rusty iron, old packing tin and tattered tarpaulin. In the house Mary draped boxes with gathered curtains of cretonne. Bob made a chest of drawers from butter boxes. Saucers of water were put on the floor at the base of the table to stop the ants climbing up.

The mosquitoes, though, were a dreadful trial; not so troublesome during the day but at night they swarmed. Bob would examine the inside of the mosquito-curtain to ensure that no insect was hiding there and then he would dash quickly into bed and tuck the curtain securely around. Often just as Mary and Bob were going to sleep, a buzzing would begin and hope of a peaceful night was finished.

One morning Mary thought that Bob had gone mad. He was jumping all over the bed like a kangaroo, his brawny arms outstretched. Mary had heard that the heat sometimes turned men delirious. But no, he was simply stalking a mosquito.

Mary never let laziness and fatigue interfere with duty. She baked, sewed, mended and gardened; made marmalade from the other Mrs Watson's recipe — the much referred to mother; loaded the new shelves with tins full of shortbread and biscuits, jars of homemade preserves and pickles; lined some walls of the granite cottage with old sails to stop the mildew in the wet season; and baked date scones — although they weren't so nice without butter. Much time was spent reading new books and re-reading favourites.

She tried to tame a lizard. Mary wrote to Miss Moore that unlike snakes, lizards had earholes and eyelids. She didn't walk around much alone. She knew her fear was irrational, but when she saw those huge reptiles, large and terrifying, looking up from the rocks, moving towards her with motionless eyes, she shuddered. It brought out some primitive terror in her. What was she doing in this

119

ancient world, this souvenir land from a bygone age, this ominous but beautiful island which had been cut off from forces of change and evolution?

Mary was a woman who was quick to respond to a challenge. She certainly had enough to combat. There was something atavistic about this island, constantly harking back to the era before man, before houses. Here she had lots of scope to demonstrate her capability to overcome trouble.

A strong individual, Mary had an indomitable spirit which fed on deep-seated inner convictions regarding the meaning of life and her place in it. She was happier and more secure when doing something, than when she had, for any reason — such as idling in Cooktown — to sit without a chance of contributing to events.

She helped to establish civilization and routine on this island which was not then meant for man and she did it with zest. Oh, what pleasure she got in planning paths where none had ever been, putting hooks on a door for dressing gowns, creating modern order out of nothing. Sometimes the rustling of the bush and birds and the lap of the sea were inaudible and she felt a weird solemn stillness. The sky, blue, cloudless, lifeless, radiating from the fierce searching light of the tropical sun, was quiet until an eagle appeared, circling, circling, looking for prey. Finally it would disappear to reappear almost immediately with a small lizard in its mouth. Victor and captive would then cross the sky to adjoining Eagle Islet, jammed with nests. How odd it was amidst this continuing world of thousands of centuries to worry about the need to make a place for every-

thing, to give patterns where there had been none; the satisfaction of having a desk with pigeon holes.

Work for whites in the Queensland tropics was hard; sometimes lassitude took over and action demanded a knee-straightening initial effort. It was impossible for Mary to lie around on her island paradise. God cursed Aryans with a belief that a human being is only worthwhile if busy. Doing, doing, doing. The blacks were 'dreadful lazy creatures'.

Provisions were hard to store and to keep fresh. They were treasured and stretched so they would last until the next expedition to Cooktown. Insects won one battle in the kitchen. Unable to prevent weevils inhabiting the flour bins Mary simply baked them in her cooking. Bob, unaware of dark specs in cakes and bread, did not know that he was following the blacks by eating creepy-crawlies. It was one of Mary's many secret jokes. Baked weevils were tasteless. Mildew grew on the salt beef and mutton but that she scraped off before Bob noticed. Rice was safer to store but Mary and Bob seldom ate it — that was the food of the Chinese who were considered infinitely inferior to white settlers. Silver fish ate books and clothes; cockroaches devoured boots or any article made of leather. An extensive wardrobe was an anxiety. Small lizards and geckoes who lived in the undersides of sheets of corrugated iron, scorched hot in the sun, ran across the walls of the huts. Occasionally a scorpion would be found under some rubbish. Armies of small brown ants would appear from nowhere the moment a morsel of food was dropped and would carry crumbs away.

Mary liked Ah Sam and Ah Leong who came from Kwang-Tung Province. They wore blue pyjamas and shaved their heads naked except for a patch at the back from which they twisted their long hair into huge pigtails, coiled beneath immense pyramid hats. Always inscrutable, always busy, they were neatly dressed in short jackets and bulky trousers. She tried not to treat them in the usual maternal, patronizing 'missey-boy' way of most white settlers. Using pidgin English made Mary feel she was talking to babies.

It was said that you had to have an undeveloped sense of smell coupled with a great sense of humour to get on with the Chinese, let alone understand them. Their garlic-laden breath, together with vague smells of incense from joss-sticks, old dried fish, oyster and soya sauce, pork barbecued with coriander and garlic clung to their clothes. But they were artful. They laboured harder and more persistently than any race on earth; when they got money they somehow kept it.

The Chinese who came to Australia, to Cooktown, could not be assimilated. Their practices seemed topsy-turvy to the white settler. Absurd. 'Everything is upside down', Bob said when they were sitting outside one night — he with his tobacco, Mary with her knitting. 'In England a woman enters a room before a man. In China she takes a back seat in everything. Even when she speaks to a man

121

she stands up to show respect. Women are inferior in China. Even at a Chinese wedding the bridegroom is the centre of attraction — the bride only gets a few glances to see what sort of a bargain the family made in getting her. The bride goes to live with her husband's family. Downtrodden she is. Footbinding is an example of their attitude to women...'

It was when he was talking in a knowledgeable way about something that Mary showed admiration for her new husband. Sometimes, though, his theories were indeed odd.

'The reason for all the Chinese energy', he suggested, 'is that they are better nourished than Europeans. Centuries ago forests in China were cleared away so they could grow great areas of crops. But there wasn't enough fuel left, only a bit of dung from oxen, a few twigs. So they chopped food up and cooked it rapidly because of this shortage of fuel — too many people and too few trees; they didn't cook the goodness out of food the way the English do!'

'But you get frightful indigestion if food is raw', Mary said.·

'Not, though', answered Bob, 'if it is chopped up finely to break down fibres and then fried quickly. Their passion for culinary skills comes from being such a hungry race. Starving often. Every morsel was valuable, pampered. Just look at the spices and herbs the Chinese use instead of English pepper and salt!'

Oh, how Mary tried not to be patronizing. But when she smelt the

Charlotte Street, Cooktown (John Oxley Library)

joss-sticks of Ah Leong or Ah Sam or asked about their families, or Kwang-Chow-foo, the Dragon Throne, the 500 temples in Canton, the world-famous Yehonala, the Emperor's concubine, she found she was forcing conversation. They were, after all, so foreign. The Great Wall of China refused to crumble; barriers were too great.

Mary was glad 'the chows' were around though, not that she admitted she was ever scared of being alone if Bob was absent fishing. When the hush of the bush became oppressive she blocked it out by singing and humming songs. She looked forward to company, yet she never once admitted, not even in her secret diary, that she was lonely. Indeed, she had become fond of her domain. The few passing crews of ships provided a welcome relief from the tedium of the routine scraping for existence. She anxiously recorded the fact if an expected passing ship did not anchor. Twice in 1881 Mary went in the lugger with Bob to Cooktown to sell the *bêche-de-mer*, and to collect mail and provisions.

She looked forward to going to Cooktown, but once there she craved for home. Even though Cooktown was her only chance to practise the piano, there was something to get back to on Lizard Island; the hens hatching eggs, birds that came at dusk, the nightly ritual of pouring water in a bowl on a platform that Ah Sam had hammered onto a branch of a Casuarina tree.

The name of her island home reminded Mary of Cornwall, Lizard Head. The last memory of the Motherland. The *City of Agra*. And then Mary would push away all thought of it, for The Lizard is a haunted place. That wasn't why Captain Cook had christened this island so. He had named it because of the multitude of four-legged reptiles. Or had he? She switched her mind.

Newlyn, even St Newlyna's Church and the fig tree with its curses, seemed remote. That scene of cosy elegant comfort and good cheer; Sunday dinner when twelve always sat down at the table; the smell of freshly baked bread in the morning; young Bill bringing in the pail of milk through the oak kitchen door; Papa listening to her practising the piano; the crispness of the pages of new books; strawberries and cream. Then the debts, the disorder; the chaotic sadness. First the trades people who had become a little pressing. Then Miss Moore with her face of ancient ivory who had smiled knowingly and said, 'I am giving you a scholarship'. Mary forced herself to stop recalling the past.

Chapter Fourteen

The Dream and the Reality

Lizards do not need to drink. They quench their thirst by staying very still for a few hours and absorbing the liquid they require through the pores of their scaly skin. Whereas humans perspire lizards absorb moisture from the air. So the water shortage late every winter on Lizard Island was only a disadvantage to intruders, not to cold-blooded reptiles. The island had fresh water in three places: a brackish stream emptying into the sea, a swampy pool with good drinking water slightly behind the stream, and a natural well near another bay. Near the swamp Captain Watson cultivated the well-furrowed patch called The Farm about 200 yards away from the cottage. Ah Leong grew 'weleables' — tomatoes, cabbages, sweet potato, pumpkin, turnip, corn — as well as tropical fruits — bananas, paw-paws and mangoes.

Ah Sam's duties in the house included keeping three kerosene-tin buckets in the kitchen full of water from the well and filling a few other buckets from the brackish stream for the laundry copper. He also dug new lavatory holes every month at the back of the house and moved the corrugated iron privies over them: one for the whites and one for the Chinese. He kept the wicks in the kerosene lanterns trimmed, scrubbed pots and pans in the sand and bolted the shutters at night over the glassless windows. During one cyclone trees had been uprooted and the smoke-house blown away. Being in the trade-wind belt meant that tremendous gusts raced across Lizard Island. Constant was the toil of sawing and chopping mangrove branches ready for the smoking fire for the *bêche-de-mer,* and hacking up the roots of trees to make way for gardens.

The winds, weather and the garden became Mary's obsession: winds controlled the coming and going of fishing expeditions, money, the safety and the number of days she would be alone. The diary entries that she forced herself to write every night were frequently nothing more than weather reports; often simply, 'Bob to the Barrier; good tank of fish'.

Many sailors and fishermen perished in the waves along the Great Barrier Reef — the seas around are watery graves filled with corpses and shipwrecks. At low tide strings of shoals, sand cays and reefs stretch endlessly like stepping stones in shallow waters. At high tide they disappear from sight, turning the sea into a nightmare of hazards for ships.

One night in January during the heat and monsoonal rain, Bob's boat had not returned. Mary wrote, 'I went up to the top of the first big hill. No sign of the cutter. Sat up until 11 p.m. Feel very nervous. Dogs barking constantly.'

What a relief it always was when Mary saw the cutter zig-zagging towards the island, its full spread of canvas out. At the first sight of it Mary rushed and put on her hessian apron, Ah Sam lit the wood fire, filled the tanks with buckets of salt water and with Ah Leong's help got it on the boil ready for the *bêche-de-mer*. The giant cauldron was half a four-foot square water-tank. The sacks of wriggling sea-slugs were hauled off the boat and thrown into the cauldron. After being boiled for twenty to thirty minutes, each one was taken out, slit open, gutted and then dried in the sun for a few days. The final process was smoking when the slugs were placed on wire racks and dried in the smoke-house for one to two days. The wood used contributed flavour, the best being the red mangrove. Finally when they looked like charred sausages, the sea-slugs were bagged, sent to Cooktown and shipped to China.

Some nights, after the slugs were cured, Bob and Mary would sit on the sand in the moonlight, the sea in front of them, his hand over her hand, planning their future. They would go 'home' to Scotland to see his mother and then to Cornwall to see Mary's relatives. Just for a holiday. But first to Sydney to ride on the tram-cars and shop in the giant department stores. And Mary would have a piano. Not a grand one from Collard and Collard but a piano nevertheless.

Mary was pregnant. Three months before the baby was due she went to Cooktown — many women left alone in remote parts of Australia died in childbirth, while desperate husbands rushed off on horses or in boats to fetch help.

Bob, who was not there, need not have worried. After a four-hour labour on 3 June, Thomas Ferrier was born in the house rented from Mr Matthews up on the hill. Mary wrote in her diary:

'Had to send Fanny (the temporary maid) away about 6.00 p.m. for Mrs Boland (the fortnightly nurse). Thomas Ferrier born ten to 11.00 p.m. Only Mrs Boland and myself in the house, no doctor required. Watch and robes from Rockhampton. 12 months today landed with Carrie on the Lizard.

Cooktown

4th Saturday. Things all right, self well as could be expected. No visitors.
5th Sunday. Self and Ferrier getting on well. Mrs Napier called to see me.
6th Monday. Mrs Matthews and Mr Hartley came to see the baby. Self and baby pretty well. No strangers.
7th Tuesday. Self getting on excellently also Ferrier. No visitors. Fanny Jones gone home. Nellie her sister came instead. Suits me much better...

And so the entries continue. Alone in Cooktown. The new baby. No family, no husband to comfort and cheer. Just a few casual friends to fill the void. Thirteen long days and nights were endured by Mary before Captain Watson came to see his son. While waiting — every minute after every hour, every day after that long week — Mary was depressed. On 16 June she wrote, 'Not quite so well as usual. Furiously watching the flag staff. Very cold and blowing hard. Mrs Boland very unwell. Not able to come down. Her time expired today. Ferrier all right. Mr Matthews nailed up a piece of tin to my bedroom window.'

It was odd having to get Mr Matthews to board up the window. But she had this subliminal feeling of dread; something terrifying. Always she slept with a box of matches and a pistol under her pillow — the matches for the candle and the pistol for the intruder — but

126

the fear enveloped her. It would be better when Bob came. Where was he?

He sailed in on 19 June with Mr Fuller. Four days later Ferrier was christened by Father Hachett at the Roman Catholic Church. Mary wrote, 'Mrs Boland godmother. Bob and priest godfathers; self did not go. Out today for the first time...'

They sailed back to Lizard Island on 29 June. '...Ferrier very good. The sea did not affect him. Self sick. Mrs Cootes came down to the wharf with her baby. Mrs Bliss lent me a chair while waiting at the wharf for Bob...'

The Aborigines were winning the Lizard Island battle, although they were not yet aware of approaching victory. Captain Watson was preparing to leave the island. The seas around were becoming fished out; the catches of *bêche-de-mer* being boiled in the old tank and stirred by the dis-used rowing paddles were smaller each week.

Mary was at the sewing machine when he first told her about his plan. He had his hair brushed, his pipe filled and lighted, his shirt sleeves rolled up to the elbows. He wiped his hand across his nose as he always did when nervous. She caught sight of herself in the mirror — a perfect frow and fright! He hadn't the courage to tell her when face to face so he stood behind her.

He told her of his intention to settle on Night Island, about 200 miles north of Lizard Island. He explained, '...the lack of sea-slugs around Lizard Island... Fished out now. Night Island an infinitely better prospect... it lay as close to the Great Barrier Reef as Lizard Island...The nesting ground for thousands of Torres Strait pigeons...' Mary reluctantly agreed but could she and the baby remain behind while Bob and Mr Fuller went to Night Island on a preparatory expedition?

At the time this seemed sensible. Mary would be safer on Lizard Island than risking a sea voyage with a newly born baby to an as yet unexplored destination.

Soon the lugger was careened on the beach in preparation for Bob's departure; a week was spent defouling it and then, on 1 September, when the baby was three months old, Mr Fuller and Captain Watson set off for the settlement's prospective new home. So began another departure-arrival cycle in the nomadic life that most immigrants had to follow, in search of a place that would fulfil their needs. Lizard Island had been found wanting; the hunt had to be resumed. On and on.

In six to eight weeks time the men would return, before the hot weather and the crisp south-easterlies which preceeded the monsoon. They might be in their new home by Christmas. Bob kept Mary and Ferrier in focus through binoculars as the cutter disappeared into the ever-retreating horizon.

Mary sat on the beach — her beach — picking up shells, throwing them up into the air and watching them make dents in the sand. If only this time everything worked out for Bob. She thought of him on the deck; sea to him was like land to her. His time away from the sea had been unhappy. He needed to breathe salt air, to feel the pitch of a boat on water. She didn't like being on the sea; it made her uneasy and nauseous. In the Great Barrier Reef she was also scared of sharks.

As the *Isabella*, named after Bob's mother, zig-zagged around the reefs Bob looked at the clear, blue sea. He had a presentiment that something was wrong. He shouldn't have left Mary and the baby. If only he didn't have to go, but the three of them had to eat. Pioneer life was dominated by the aphorism 'Better luck, next time, mate!' The quest.

Mary looked out over the same endless sea, evening after evening. Here she was on this mountainous island set apart from the world by vast areas of water; that estranging sea which isolated her. Ah Sam and Ah Leong rarely even spoke pidgin English; mostly they giggled and chattered away with attitudes and a language that she never understood. She could talk and listen to them but never have a conversation. The naked savages who prowled in the background of her life were mere shadows and sounds; not understanding them, she ignored them. She was disturbed at the idea of being uprooted, having to create another home on another island. Her effort in making Lizard Cottage comfortable had been enormous.

She hoped that Ferrier would not need medical attention while Bob was away. What would she do then? There was not even a dinghy on the island as Bob had said that as she could neither sail nor swim well, a boat would be dangerous. The reefs, shoals and sharks demanded expert sailors who either knew where the deeps were or who had charts. Signalling a passing boat with fires or flags from a cairn was Mary's only link with the world, a world cut off by an impassable tropic sea.

A surveying party from H.M.S. *Fly* in 1843 had erected a cairn of rocks at the highest point of the island as an aid to ships charting passages and reefs. Sometimes Mary had climbed up the 1,200 feet with Bob. She liked to see the Coral Sea waves thundering in and breaking on the Great Barrier Reef. There was also another cairn of rocks on the lower hill near a hollow sheltered by large boulders where she could be protected in all weathers.

Sometimes Mary saw a boat in the distance. The channel to Cook's Passage was the route from Melbourne and Sydney to Japan, the Dutch Indies, China, the Philippines and Singapore. A few times when she saw a ship in the distance it made her feel deeply alone; her eyes would fill with tears — visions came before her of happy people on board — in the Great Cabin after dinner when it was filled with music and talk and togetherness. For the steam boats were far superior in luxury to the sailing ships. It was difficult alone; sometimes she felt frustrated but there was a wonderful feeling of scope to develop in the freedom of this different, appealing primitive world. She thought of the convention-ridden society of England.

Contrasting with her competitive pioneer spirit were strong maternal feelings, and so, despite her active, impatient nature, Mary enjoyed caring for Ferrier. His birth had diminished her desire to go back to Cooktown. The mainland was not the safest place for small babies; miners sometimes died of typhoid, cholera, dysentery and influenza. Thousands of white settlers had migrated to cemeteries, not homes.

Ferrier

It was easier to feel the warmth of friendship from a distance; friends that only took up the time of writing or reading a letter or contemplation — one could have close friends who did not bore one or clutter up the day. Mary decided that social activity in a new town is often exhausting because no rituals of acceptance have been established. And loneliness made people too familiar too quickly. Oh, yes, she rationalized, here on Lizard Island friendships do not deteriorate through contact and boredom and repetition and nothingness. Letters could be highlights.

Music, though, had no substitute. She missed the sound of melodies to fill the silences, to elate her. The old music box with the wind-up key was now very worn and sounded like a third-rate circus chorus. She thought of the telephone. The first public exchange had been installed in London the year before they had left England. Surely, though, the telephone made one feel more lonely, just the voice without the presence. Voices that could travel, leave the body behind. A voice that flew like a bird, that made sound abstract. She had read of the invention of the phonograph that could bring an orchestra — by a scratch that made a noise — into everyday life, into the kitchen.

Mary tried to argue away the silence — or was it loneliness, her need to say something and to get another response? I am, she thought, just like the lizards who are solitary creatures and seldom form colonies. So many things are said aloud to another person which might just as well never have been spoken, remarks passed simply to make links with another person. So many sentences might as well have been said standing in front of a mirror, words spoken when just seeking something — reassurance, praise, a ticket away from loneliness. She wrote scores of unposted letters — the outlet of a woman who had no one to talk to.

When the sad reality came with the tears, she knew all this pondering was twaddle. Utter twaddle. She had to remain on Lizard Island because she did not have enough money to live on once she got to Cooktown. Bob had only managed to give her £2 when he left. But she had provisions and Ah Sam and Ah Leong netted fish over at the lagoon. And she was proud.

All day Mary chattered away to Ferrier as she did her chores, voicing her thoughts aloud. She talked on, whether he gurgled or not, wiping his hot forehead from time to time with her handkerchief. Being so alone made her more and more dependent on the baby. Some days she had a feeling of solitude; some days a despair of loneliness. She had no distraction from maternal devotion, no one else who had to be fed and listened to, no one around to dilute the atmosphere between mother and son. No one to notice that her cuticles were creeping up and her fingernails needed filing, no one to stop her reading books. She missed Bob, or was it the presence of a familiar person she missed? Anyway she adjusted and liked the respite from his moods. Although he would never even admit to himself that he would suffer jealousy, Bob was envious of the attentions she poured on Ferrier. One advantage of Bob's absence was less washing, ironing and cooking. Instead of changing the sheets on the bed every Saturday she turned them around to save washing a sheet only half slept on.

At dusk every night Mary sat — carefully covered in her insect repellant of citronella oil and lavender — under the Casuarina trees as the birds flew down to drink and eat her left-over bread. When she had been alone for twenty-two days a wind blew up. She gazed at the water breaking in white foam on the hard white sand and the contrast of the deep Prussian blue of the sea and the light green and brown of the water over the reef. Her mind turned to the England she missed. She saw the hyacinth in the grass, a magnolia tree in bud and the daffodils in all the glory of the late winter's sunshine. She heard her father's approbation after she played the organ at church and she heard a thrush singing on a frosty morning.

'Everything in Australia is upside down compared to England', Mary told Ferrier. 'The man in the moon is upside down; when it is day here, it is night there; when it is summer here, it is winter there. Swans in Australia are black; eagles are white; native bees don't sting; cuckoos coo in the night; owls screech in the day. North winds are hot and south winds cold; fur-covered animals live in water and lay eggs and suckle their young; birds with giant wings cannot fly; in England my shadow falls towards the north at noon, but here my shadow falls towards the south; some animals hop instead of run; gum trees shed bark as well as leaves; the male emu hatches the eggs instead of the mother bird; when the English are eating dinner at night we are eating breakfast. In Australia Christmas is one of the hottest days of the year, in England it is one of the coldest. One day, my darling, you too will have a Christmas in Cornwall and after roast turkey we will all sit around the cosy fire in the same room, in the same house, in the same town where your great-grandfather enjoyed fifty Christmases.'

A fondness for all the old places she had left overcame her; her home near the other Lizard. The only things from the past, the constants in her life, were her old tin trunk, the bible, the watch her father had given her and the moon, the sun and some of the stars. The stars. A European who migrates to the antipodes will never see the bright Northern Star, the Polaris, again; a different sphere of heaven is above. Polaris is exclusive to the northern hemisphere whereas the Southern Cross floats up and can be seen from places north of the equator.

131

Chapter Fifteen

The
Medicine Man

The medicine man, by means of invisible ropes, could climb up and down between earth and sky for he was made by supernatural beings. When he flew into the sky at night he communicated with the spirits who could produce a condition of frenzy in the damned below. Inter-spirit etiquette is punctilious.

When in bed under her net Mary heard astonishing noises. Imaginary? No, the dogs were barking. Ghostly echoes filled silences. The sounds gave her a feeling of desperate aloneness; it was fear, the sort of fear that made hands moist and spines alert. She had crossed twenty-three days off the calendar since Bob had sailed away. Perhaps this solitary life had driven her mad? No, no, no. Mary got up as soon as daylight crept in through the crevices in the granite and coral walls; the sun always gave her the feeling of safety and freshness. As soon as she lit the kerosene primus stove to make dawntime tea, routine took over from fright; sheer physical activity blocked thought and worry. She crossed another day off the calendar. It was the only way of knowing whether it was Tuesday or Sunday. Then she checked the boxes of matches in the tin. Her horror was to find she had run out, or that they had got too wet to light and she would have no fire.

She was always reading or bustling; the house and the baby had to be clean and tidy. Housework was pursued with zest; it gave the day shape and purpose, and scrupulous cleanliness in the tropics kept down the level of ants, cockroaches, weevils and flies. A person alone has more energy than a person in a crowd — the space around the person alone acts almost as bellows to a fire.

When she was alone there was really nothing to stop her staying in bed all day, or staying up all night — the rhythm of community life set up by what Papa called the need to exchange, was no longer.

Instead the need for survival, the need of Bob's praise when he came back, and the irritating human satisfaction derived from habit and continuity took over. She started to sing. Although it seemed a sign of madness to voice sentences to herself, to sing aloud was sane. Keep busy, do not think. Sing loud and stop thoughts going round and round in your head. She decided not to write them down any more. For by voicing thoughts or putting them into words they become real.

A never-ending war was waged against the insects — as well as the Aborigines — for possession of the Queensland Tropics. Night and day thousands of insects were crawling, chewing, sucking, biting and boring away at plants in gardens or the fabric of houses — even the foundations. Also there was the constant battle with herself: so many emigrant women, debilitated by heat and humidity, became slovenly. They lolled around, bedazed by the sun or enervated by the months of drought or flood. And there was always the dust. Sea breezes could turn to gales, blowing dirt and sand through cracks in the cottage and covering everything with a fine layer of sand or dirt.

On 26 September Mary had boiled her Christmas puddings and hung them in calico cloths on hooks in the kitchen. The only Christmas ingredient that had not been imported to the colony of Queensland was snow: recipes, customs and games were transported. Christmas cakes, puddings, mince pies, Christmas trees with presents, cards and carols were relished. By observing English customs the new settlers could temporarily pretend they were at home. It was really too early to make the pudding, but the urge to start the feast preparations was so strong, that Mary argued that the ants might get into the dried fruit if she left it any longer. There was so little that was continuous in her life. She poured extra brandy into the mixture to help preserve the puddings during the hot months and thought, 'God help the Good Templars!'

She remembered that it was the 26th of September — the anniversary of the dedication of the Church of St Newlyna. The fig tree sprouting out of the wall would soon be losing its leaves with the approaching winter. Mary put the yeast in the wash-house to rise...What was it? Something was wrong. It's just the blacks, she thought, a lot of canoes had come over earlier that day. From time to time she could hear the Aborigines yelling. Or was it the lizards? It was impossible to live in a state of chronic apprehension so she tried to ignore the noises. It was only a few days after the Spring Equinox and already lizards were stetching out of their long winter hibernation. She tried to think of something more concrete: the goats had gone dry — almost a relief she was so bored with goat's milk. Monday, washday.

It was 7 p.m., dark and noisy with the shrill of cicadas. 'Oh, the peg bag is still hanging on the clothesline', Mary muttered to Ferrier, in her usual way of voicing aloud all her thoughts. She was about to retrieve it when she heard weird resonant tappings, moans and gurgles coming from the hill. The noise ceased: then it came again until drowned by the tide on the warm sand. Then again — louder.

What was it? She didn't go to the yard to get the peg bag. A chilling emotion overcame her.

The medicine man squatted on his haunches, chanting the prescribed song. Suddenly he jerked the death-bone in the direction of his old victim: Mrs Watson. Extreme care was taken as he pointed the bone lest its evil power recoil on him: the sun and the moon were behind him; the waterhole was not in between him and his target. As he recited the fateful incantations he re-inforced his original spell of death.

A more potent weapon than a spear, the death-bone is a human bone scraped and rubbed to a tapering point. At one end a fine plait of human hair is cemented; at the other end another but longer plait is attached to a larger, hollow human bone. When the stiletto-shaped bone is directed towards an individual the curse of death begins. But if the black sorcerer begins to tremble at the end of the ceremony he knows something is amiss and his only chance of throwing off the evil spell is immediately to jump into a waterhole with the bone in his hand.

The flare from the candle fixed in its own wax on a saucer was burning unevenly and gave a wan light. The baby was asleep under Mary's mosquito net; she was trying to read by candlelight — if she lit the hurricane light it would attract too many insects. She thought she heard something tip-toeing outside — or someone? Blackfellow or possum? She poured a glass of water from the floral jug on the rickety wash-stand and stood gazing at the inside of the cottage. On the wall was a framed lithograph of a grand carriage with eight horses driving through a Scottish snow storm. Bob had often told her where it was in the moors, but she always forgot; Lossiemouth? Lochness?

Suddenly she stood aghast and for an unknowing reason raised her arms in horror. Her eyes became glassy and went into a fixed stare; she was transfixed. She attempted to scream but the sound choked in her throat. Her body trembled and the muscles moved involuntarily. She swayed backwards and forwards in a swoon until she fell to the ground. She lay there writhing as if in mortal agony, covering her face with her hands. She went into a faint. When she woke the candle had gone out. For the first time in her life she climbed into bed fully clothed, seeking the protection of the fine white mosquito net. She did not know that high on the hill the medicine man had pointed the bone at her.

The death-bone had not worked before as she had been with her husband; telepathy and thought waves only reach those who are silent. It is when alone that a man hears ghosts, has visions, for the human brain and body can only receive a number of messages at once. When people are in a group, thought waves are diluted but when they are alone for long periods the spirits have room to rush in. Telepathic messages more easily touch the nerve ends and penetrate the speech centres of the brains of people who are alone or of people who are quiet and still within themselves than people who are living with others. Just as people who go blind develop a compensatory sensitivity to touch and smell, people who are isolated develop a heightened power to communicate with people at a distance.

Mary frowned as she woke at dawn. 'Why am I not in my nightdress?' She lay looking through the mosquito net. Something awful had happened but recall wouldn't bring it back. The south-easterly came blowing steadily up from the mainland. Mary wrote: 'Tuesday. Blowing gale of wind SE. Ah Sam saw smoke in S direction. Supposed to be from native camp. Steamer bound north very close, about 6 p.m. *Corea,* I think.'

Wednesday has the shortest entry in the whole diary: 'Strong SE breeze.' Nothing else.

On Thursday Ah Leong was dead. But Mary's diary reveals no horror, no fear, no sadness: 'Blowing strong SE, although not so hard as yesterday. No eggs. Ah Leong killed by the blacks over at the farm. Ah Sam found his hat which is the only proof.'

The heavy wooden door of the cottage was barred that night. When the weird noises came closer Mary put the rifle to the loophole near the key. The dogs were inside and howling. Ferrier was crying.

On Friday, the fifth night of the eerie rituals and invisible siege, the natives crept along the beach close to the cottage. Again Mary put the rifle up to the loop-hole and this time she fired high — not to kill, just to disperse. She did not shoot at them directly in case they retaliated by ransacking the cottage.

'Friday September 30. Natives down on the beach at 7 p.m. Fired off the rifle and revolver and they went away.'

Death was not Mary's only darkness; it was also fear of kidnap. Every white woman on the Queensland coast knew the savage story of Scotswoman Barbara Thompson who, shipwrecked on a reef in the north in 1842, was taken by natives after her husband had drowned and for four years was a captive wife of old Boroto. She was forced to have sexual intercourse with him. She lived with other tribal wives of this elder and never wore any clothes. They made her climb trees by applying burning sticks to her thighs and legs. There had also been Mrs Fraser who had been kidnapped near Maryborough. And others. Their long hair was cut off and used to make fish nets.

Later the Aborigines returned and Mary unbolted the shutters and defiantly stood in front of them. Inch by inch the pistol was

135

raised and pointed at a middle branch of the Casuarina tree on the beach. Her hand trembled violently. She fired. One. Two. Three. Four. Five. The natives ran towards the hill — all except the old man wearing a loin apron of emu feathers. He stood, defiant. Graceful he certainly was with long, thin limbs and fine hands; but ugly too — his face had a projecting jaw, his nose was wide and flat with human bones and cockatoo feathers stuck through a hole in its centre, his lips protruded. Strings of shark and crocodile teeth hung from his ears. A necklace of kangaroo teeth decorated his chest, grooved with deep incised scars. He stared at a lizard — a fat-stomached one covered in small brown scales — moving across the clearing. Like a snake with legs and arms, the lizard made Mary shudder. And she shuddered, too, at the dandy's scars.

Again Mary barricaded herself in. Darkness made the cottage a place of gloom; heat and stuffiness made it like hell. How she longed for a breeze. By Saturday fresh water was short so Ah Sam walked towards the farm with kerosene-tin buckets balancing on each end of a bamboo pole across his shoulders. Ambush was swift — spears came from the eucalypts above the scrub. He dropped the buckets and ran back. 'Missey, missey, 'elp...'elp!' he yelled.

Blacks hurled seven spears into his arms and shoulders, piercing with the skill they used when harpooning turtles. Hearing screams, Mary put Ferrier under the first thing she saw, the rocking chair, got to the window and fired the pistol into the air. One. Two. Three. Four. Five.

She eased the door open wide enough for Ah Sam to enter. As soon as he was in she pushed wooden trunks across it. The cottage was so dark with everything closed that Mary lit the hurricane lamp so she could see to jerk the stone spearheads out of Ah Sam's flesh. Each spear was about three feet in length and decorated at the grip end with tufts of bird feathers. The barbs, a delicate leaf shape, were blade-like and polished to a sharp cutting edge. Three spears were grass-tree shoots tipped with hardwood and barbed with sharks' teeth and sting-ray spikes. Blood flowed everywhere — but, thank goodness, thought Mary, it was not spurting. She ripped a bed sheet into strips and tied them tightly around the gashes to compress the two lips of the wounds together. After bathing each wound with water and tincture of myrrh she decided to suture two of the spear-holes as they were deep and bleeding heavily. With coarse thread and a curved upholstery needle from her sewing box Mary hem-stitched the wounds, tying the threads in bows. Ah Sam's pain was terrible. Mary found his long pipe and the small curved wooden box that he, like his dead friend Ah Leong and so many Chinese, used as a pillow. She took a stick of opium tobacco from the box, put it in the wooden pipe and lit it with a cinder stick off the primus stove. Ah Sam's pulse was slow, he would not have strength to draw the pipe to burn, so Mary put it in her mouth and inhaled. The sickening taste of the burning poppy seeds in the back of her throat made her

Remains of the cottage, Lizard Island

swallow hard; she inhaled again and transferred the pipe to Ah Sam's thin lips. He drew. Habit took over. After half an hour his pulse rate increased; he smiled before falling into a protracted sleep.

The heat and dry nervous air in the sealed up cottage was oppressive and caused breathlessness — the sort that kept her mouth gaping. Dipping a mug in the bucket of water to quench Ferrier's thirst Mary noticed it was only half full. The ambushed buckets abandoned near the farm were needed desperately. A bucket of brackish water — used for washing — was near the wash-house outside. Yes, Mary would risk it. She ran as if pursued, picked up the bucket and retraced her eight steps back to the front door. Spears came down towards her face. She looked up and ducked to miss them. They had not been aimed to kill but to frighten. She was not sure why but she picked up the spears before retreating inside and bolting the door. After putting the precious bucket of water near the stove Mary rushed to Ferrier, pulling him out from under the chair. She was crying. Shaking. Screaming. Raving. She realized she must pull herself together. The urge to do something with those fidgety hands, anything, was immediate. She found an old copy of the Cooktown *Courier* and used it to wrap the three spears which she did, as she did most things, with the baby tucked under her right arm. She put the spear bundles under the bed to show Bob when he returned.

'Natives (4) speared Ah Sam; four places in the right side and three in the shoulder. Got three spears from the natives. Saw 10 men altogether.'

Here the pencil stopped.

137

Chapter Sixteen

Escape from Lizard Island

There was a new moon that Saturday night and the sky was darker than black. Mary could not see but she could feel the lively eyes of natives when she squinted out through the loop-hole of the door. The opium had sent Ah Sam to sleep. He was still bleeding from the wounds inflicted by the seven spears earlier that day, but not so heavily. The invalid's inscrutable expression masked whether the opium had blocked the throbbing and the pain.

The temperature in the room, now airless from lack of ventilation, caused perspiration to drip down Mary's face as she fanned the baby. Apart from the death of Ah Leong, the stabbing of Ah Sam and natives lurking in the foliage, another fear, a peculiar horror, still gripped Mary. If the house were older she might have said it was haunted, but it had only been built three years ago. She shuddered. She was unaware that whenever a tribe member dies his spirit goes back to sacred ground until he chooses to be reincarnated. Nor did she know that lizards were reincarnations, 'the men made out of nothing' — Ungambikula — descending from the sky.

Mary tried to divert her mind from darkness with a practical problem: survival. Walls and floor closed round. Was the brackish water fit to drink? She took the small bottle of Condy's Crystals, dropped a little into a cup of water and waited. If it became pink it meant that the water was safe: if it turned brown it was dangerous. The water turned brown. The sediment was thick and the water could not even be used for washing until it had stood for a day. Return to the waterhole would probably mean death by spear or boomerang. Impossible to risk it. A few inches of water in the tank beside the house which collected the gutter water off the roof would have been enough but it had not rained for months. The tank, like

138

the ground and the grass, was parched as it usually was at the end of the dry warm tropical winter. The monsoonal rains proper would not bring the wet till December or January. One of those early odd storms would save the situation. Or Bob. 'Cry for help', a voice inside her urged. She yelled, but only in her head.

She tried to remain calm. She had been known to be a sensible girl, a girl who could cope, a teacher who had frequently told her pupils, 'Come on, none of this nonsense'. It was the 1st of October; Bob would not return for ten days or two weeks. If she barricaded the three of them in the house they would die of heat, lack of oxygen and thirst — if they weren't speared. A feeling of creepiness again enveloped her. People were tip-toeing outside. She felt the blacks' resentment coming in through the wall. Ferrier snuggled up under her left arm, her right hand was on the cocked pistol. All night she kept a vigil; terror stretched her eyes open. When they closed she propped open the lids with her fingers and blinked. If the natives pushed the shutters down she must be ready to shoot and defend her little garrison. Most of any battle is silence and waiting.

At last Mary saw a glimmer of sun through the cracks and crevices in the coral mortar; the fearful night was over. Daylight brought hope. Ferrier and Ah Sam still slept but the dogs wanted to get out. They might augment the threat of bullets and act as a deterrent. The natives were no longer close; well, she felt they weren't. With arms that ached from exhaustion Mary half opened a shutter so the dogs could jump out. When she looked across the bay she screamed. Weird motifs of fish, men, boomerangs, fighting picks, axes and spears had been painted in black on the smoke-house. She turned to look at the walls of the stone cottage. Signs of a tribal devil were painted on them too — stained with charcoal, white pipe-clay and blood. The natives were invoking the help of sorcery, thought Mary, to kill her and Ferrier.

But was this primitive religion with its superstition, myth and ritual really different from Cornish Christianity? Did the death-bone equal the fig tree? Man has always had religion of some sort. Even in this primitive culture, there was ritual belief in survival and the power of nature. Suddenly Mary saw the mighty law of nature underlaying all religions. All believed in an omniscient and omnipotent divine power that had brought this world and ourselves into existence. Evidence is not needed for the knowledge, she thought, it is something innate in man. Like the inborn need to eat, copulate and sleep.

It was time for the baby's feed, time to change Ah Sam's bandages. Again Mary pushed the bolt across the wooden shutters and turned the cottage into a dark, airless fortress. Outside she heard a thud. After a few hours she had to open a window to get over the suffocating effect of the heat. Queer noises of water, wind and voices. The dogs did not come back.

Escape was imperative. But how? What could be used as a raft?

Aboriginal motifs daubed on the smoke house (James Cook Museum, Cooktown)

Determined to do everything well, Mary was exact in her application to chosen tasks or duty — the self-protective intent in the resourceful escape she was plotting was coupled with a compulsive desire to maintain self-imposed standards — whatever happened.

Light broke into her brain: Danaë and Perseus had been cast out to sea in a wooden chest, Mary could use the *bêche-de-mer* cauldron and also float away and be picked up by a passing vessel. The tank was only four foot square and of dubious bouyancy, but there was no alternative. Mary thought again of going to the waterhole but knew that the Aborigines would be waiting to ambush her. Her fear of kidnap was greater than that of death. She looked out the peephole again. They had come back. Three were waiting. She shuddered at the idea of the blacks touching her, making her take her clothes off.

All over the island natives were waiting; waiting to see when the death-bone would kill the white woman. Ah Leong had already been taken to the mainland and eaten. They had baked him in the usual way — dug a big hole in the ground, lined it with stones and then filled it with fire wood which was fiercely burnt so that the stones would almost glow and would retain the heat for hours. Once the fire burnt out Ah Leong was carefully wrapped in plantain leaves and

140

was placed on the scorching stones. Ah Leong and the hole were then covered with dirt. Eight hours later the natives returned, dug away the dirt and pulled out the baked man — long pig.

Meal times and beds were unknown among Aborigines — their dinners depended not on the position of the sun in the sky but on when food was caught. They wandered around searching for food, often not knowing where they would sleep at night. They used their stomachs as cupboards to store any food they found.

Aborigines, endowed with the power of telepathy, knew the white woman was preparing to go. She would leave Lizard Island and never return so again the Ungambikula would reign on their sacred land. They waited. Up on the hill they sat cross-legged with their heels and feet drawn under them to form pillows. Beside the smoke-house the sentries stood in the stance peculiar to natives — one foot on the ground, the other foot placed against the knee so the two legs formed the shape of the capital letter P. They balanced themselves by leaning on spears or nulla-nullas.

Confusion prevailed but Mary managed to assemble what she would need for the precarious journey — picking things up, putting things down — the old cooking pot would not take much more than two adults and a baby. The baby was Mary's only comfort. All her life she had been a faithful attender at church but now her religion was no strength or solace: only the moral concepts it had inculcated earlier were a guidance. Now that she really needed God she felt no unity with him. No comfort came from repeating prayers, and 'God help me... dear Lord... Light in our Darkness...' were but hollow pleas. Instead, strange passages from the bible filled her mind with gloom: 'And fear not them which kill the body, but are not able to kill the soul. But rather fear him which is able to destroy both Soul and Body in Hell...' If only she could effect more dependence on heaven. God did not exist or he had deserted her. The devil? Had he taken over? She felt no connection when she appealed: 'We beseech Thee O Lord...' God was not with her when all morning she went backwards and forwards from the trunks and cupboards, her arms full of a mixture of things necessary and things sentimental. That God who had helped David to defeat an entire army with a rock thrown from a sling was not with her. But she packed the bible nevertheless.

Ah Sam's breathing was now regular enough for him to light his own opium pipe and the airless cottage was oppressive with the fumes. Mary took a risk and opened the shutters, the smell of sea-weed was pungent — the tide she thought must be on the ebb.

The equipment was ready: clothes, a saw, a hammer, her watch, jewellery, money (£2 and some silver coins was all she had), umbrella, bonnet, pillow, food — including tins of sardines, bread, goat's and condensed milk, a new exercise book, a new sharp pencil. The little remaining water was poured into water bags. Appalled at

141

the challenge of walking from the house to the tank and getting the tank floating far enough into the bay beyond spearing distance, she took the brown belt off her waist and strapped Ferrier onto her back with the help of a shawl tied around her neck and under her arm. The luggage, which she had tied into a bundle in a dress, she slung over her left shoulder. On the other shoulder she slung the rifle. Her hands had to be free to shoot. The pistol was in her right hand — cocked. Ah Sam stood behind her.

She opened the door; only the dandy wearing the loin apron of emu feathers stood there. She walked down the three steps and forward towards the smoke-house. The emu-feather dandy did not move. When she got to the cauldron, which was still resting on the bars across the open fire-place, she climbed in. Ah Sam scrambled after her. She lowered her bundle to the bottom of the smelly dry tank and placed the baby on the pillow. The emu man and the natives hidden in the foliage watched. All the prognostications of the medicine man were to be verified; she was going to cook herself!

Then Mary and Ah Sam scrambled out, pulled the tank towards

The tank and paddles used by Mary (Queensland Museum)

the beach and into the clear water, over the sand which shoals towards the beach — the pistol in Mary's hand, the rifle still on her shoulder. There was not far to push as high tide was just on the turn. She threw in the two rough paddles which were used as giant wooden spoons to stir the *bêche-de-mer*.

The sea-water which soaked through her long poplin dress cooled her as they pulled the tank out about twenty feet until they were waist deep in water. She held the tank to stop it capsizing while Ah Sam gripped the side and pulled himself in. Once in he counter-balanced it as Mary heaved and levered herself in, weighed down by the water in her dress and her shoes. She briskly arranged the baby on the pillow. She took one paddle and, although still terribly weak, Ah Sam took the other and they managed to get the blunt-bowed cooking pot moving away from the shore between the large coral patch and the northern headland. Never has there been such a clumsy craft, thought Mary, except for Danaë and Perseus's wooden chest. Danaë was probably the only other woman who had gone to sea with a baby in a square box with a flat bottom. Mary was re-enacting the Greek tragedy!

She did not have time to ponder. So debilitating was the effort needed to keep heaving the paddles and to keep afloat that she could not think ahead; nothing concerned her except the existing second. Now. The threat of death and danger blocks out everything — apart from the total awareness of the present. Time seemed to be withdrawn. Mary could see nothing except the sky and sea stretching away to mergence. Her South Sea island was behind — nothing but a beautiful dream.

The danger, though, was not real: the natives did not even attempt to overtake Mary in their canoes. They watched from the shore. Mary was beyond the flesh; spears were not needed to kill her. But the sea all about her was a new horror. The unkind current took the cauldron abruptly as if it was a cork so the paddles were no longer needed. Quickly they were swept along. They could go no other way now.

The last sight of Lizard Island. She had caught her last sight of the other Lizard just over four years ago; the bell tolling for souls lost in the sea.

Mary thought of all the criticism and all the clichés about the Aborigines. She had read articles in newpapers about Charles Darwin's origin of species by means of natural selection and descent of man. Life was no more than a selfish struggle of one species against another; the survival of the fittest. Darwin suggested that man had evolved on a safe island or isolated continent. Perhaps Australia? The blackfellows in Australia were the most archaic men known in the world. But they knew the land and lived in harmony with nature, unlike the European who changed what always had been. Still in the Stone Age the Aborigines were nomadic and had no

143

beasts of burden to travel on; did not sow any crops; had no pottery techniques and their weapons were sharpened stones, sticks and shells; their drinking vessels were made from beach shells or skulls, and their blankets were softened sheets of bark.

They had not invented the wheel, but neither had some sophisticated races such as the Tibetans. Even a few missionaries who had come to North Queensland with 'the love of God' had failed to befriend these wild blacks, let alone lead them along the Thoroughfare to Heaven and Jesus Christ, teach them not to beat their women with nulla-nullas and sticks, or not to continue polygamy. The native practices with women were sometimes revolting, burying a girl in a hole with dirt up to her waist for the first three menstrual periods, for five days at a stretch with no food except a specified yam — even her hands were buried so scratching was impossible. Equally revolting to the missionaries was the practice of bestowing young girls on old men as spare wives.

Darwin's theory was discussed by the white settlers; some believed that man was descended from an ape, not an angel — except for Adam, Eve and the serpent. They considered themselves educated. In this community of whites and pagan yellows and blacks, the Europeans felt their aloofness. 'We are superior', were words seldom voiced, but often thought. Racial prejudice was heightened by what they saw with their own eyes. They asserted that Caucasians represented the pinnacle of evolutionary development; other races were intrinsically inferior.

'We're just re-enacting another chapter of Social Darwinism, eh?' was a typical remark of a white colonial as he picked up his gun for a few shots at the blacks. 'The fittest have always survived and the weak and the unnecessary have become extinct. Only those varieties of life that are better fitted to their environment will continue.'

The early North Queenslanders believed in their own innate superiority; nothing was inherently wrong with dispossessing the weak. The blacks were a 'doomed race' and their 'extinction was inevitable'.

Mary remembered those mock-colonel voices at the Cooktown functions: 'Colossal, old chap... Really... Even those scientist fellows say that blacks are early examples of man. In other parts of the world they have become extinct because they were so backward. Was it thousands or millions of years ago?'

'Wasn't that new port in the Gulf of Carpentaria named after Charles Darwin because of what he said about evolution in Australia? They certainly didn't name the port after him because of what he said about Australia. He had written in his book: "Farewell Australia! I leave your shores without sorrow or regret!" '

The rationalization would be continued with the theory that varieties of man seem to act on each other in the same way as different species of animals — the stronger wiping out the weaker. It was a 'them or us' situation in a country so arid that a non-hunting white man could not survive unless he took with him his own seeds or food propagated from imported seed. They or we would lose the Darwinian struggle for survival.

It always seemed a harsh criticism to Mary that the Aborigines were considered backward because they did not cultivate crops or have any beasts of burden. What indigenous plant in Australia was palatable enough to want to grow; what animal was there that a man could ride — a kangaroo? An emu?

Even the writer Anthony Trollope, who had toured Australia twice in the 1870s, was critical of the Aborigines. With only George Eliot competing in fame with him as a living writer after Dickens died, Trollope's view on the blacks, despite its lack of sensitivity, was widely read:

> Their doom is to be exterminated; and the sooner their doom is accomplished — so that there be no cruelty — the better will it be for civilization...
>
> The white man, of course, felt that he was introducing civilization but the black man did not want civilization. He wanted fish, kangaroos, and liberty. And yet is there one bold enough to go back to the first truth and say that the white man should not have taken the land because it belonged to the black man; — or that if, since the beginning of things, similar justice had prevailed throughout the world, the world would now have been nearer the truth and honesty in its ways than it is?...
>
> Of the Australian black man we may certainly say that he has to go. That he should perish without unnecessary suffering should be the aim of all who are concerned.

As Mary sat cramped in the tank, under that wearying sunshine, fighting for her life against what now seemed like dark multitudes of assailants, she thought, 'Perhaps Anthony Trollope is right?' Until then, Mary had looked on the black nomadic hunters as yet another nuisance — poisonous snakes, blow-flies, mosquitoes, death spiders, alligators, crawling insects and the pretentious upstarts in Cooktown that she attempted to exclude from her English-like home.

Mary begun to ponder again: had Bob, had he slept with a black woman? A lubra or a gin? Had Bob... touched a lubra? Twice she had had enough dare in her to ask him but when her mouth had opened the question had not come out. According to court cases reported in Cooktown papers most fisherman had an Aboriginal woman — known as a lubra or a gin — who was kept or replaced at whim. Gins were naked except for the dried grass apron they wore, known among the white men as 'arse grass'. Boats called into islands such as Palm, Hinchinbrook and Dunk and lured the black women on board with gaudy beads. Older tribal men became pimps and traded young gins for tomahawks and a few ounces of tobacco. The crude sexual exploitation of Aboriginal women was well known: gins were even forcibly taken or kept on board boats. The existence of black concubines was a shocking blow to the sensibilities of the

145

white ladies of Cooktown who hid horror on their faces behind dainty fans and held in their corseted torsos when reading newspaper accounts of their men and those savages. The ladies never discussed what black gins did, but Mary heard a whisper that they kept their long skinny legs in the air. Once a white man slept with a gin, it was rumoured, nothing except 'black velvet' would satisfy him. So frantic were some men for black velvet that they were violent with unco-operative gins, running them down, tying them up and keeping them against their will. So great was their need that they ran the risk of being attacked by black men. Sometimes, though, gins were offered by tribes as gestures of friendship — Aborigines were polygamous — sex was for pleasure not procreation. Women had sex so frequently that it was part of daily life; some tribes did not know the connection between pregnancy and coitus. They practised effective birth control by chewing a certain red berry. A European might offer a guest the hospitality of a meal and a bed; an Aborigine might offer a meal plus a wife. But had Bob? Had he?

The iron tank drifted on.

Chapter Seventeen

On the Coral Sea

The sun quickly dried her wet clothes. A feeling of well-being came over Mary. She was free. Raising the green umbrella she fastened the handle onto her back with her belt to make an awning so that she was perpetually shaded from the fierce sun which so easily burnt and blistered. Ferrier snuggled up to her as she sang to him. 'Rock a-bye-baby in the tree top...' On she sang, 'When the wind blows the cradle will rock...' She broke into laughter, the laughter that links horror and amusement. Then she stopped. It was not that absurd. She had unconsciously broken into the nursery rhyme: 'Rubbity, rub, Dubbity, dub, three men in a tub... the butcher, the baker, the candlestick maker...' Ferrier held a string of her bonnet.

But it was absurd, beyond panic, to be cramped in this smelly old cooking pot with a baby at breast and an invalid Chinese beside her, all eyes squinting from the intense glare of the sea-water. Steering was her greatest problem. She put one giant wooden spoon at the back of the tank to act as a rudder. It took all her strength to hold it deep enough so they would get to the reef.

In late afternoon that wretched south-easterly with its dry salt-laden air was blowing strong, stirring up the sea into waves which swept against them. Whatever she did she had to ensure that Ferrier was not washed overboard. The iron tub rose up over the threatening wave crests that came foaming towards them. The baby screamed. And down again. Up again. Now nausea accompanied the pitching of the tank and its loathsome smell; Mary swallowed and heaved overboard. Vomit filled her nostrils and she could not find a handkerchief. It was like sliding up and down valleys and mountains. So much water splashed in that Ah Sam used his drinking mug to bail out — oh for a pump. The wind and the currents were now propelling Mary. The tank was out of their control. She knew she was a good four miles from the island.

The stars were half way across the sky when the calm came and Mary looked up. Everything was blackness: the water, the sky. The silence was terrible. Dawn: they were sailing towards the sunrise, closer and closer. 'Surely it is only through suffering and pain that we are strengthened', she consoled herself. Morning was a relief. Ah Sam held Ferrier while she rinsed some of the baby's things in the saltwater by trailing her hands overboard. She broke off some bread for their breakfast. Ah Sam looked the other way when she fed Ferrier; as usual once the baby was at her breast she felt peaceful. They had survived and she was thankful. The sea, dark and leaden in the night, was now blue, shining and flat by day.

To while away the time as they drifted, Mary told Ah Sam and Ferrier the story of how Danaë and her baby, Perseus, had been put out to sea in a square wooden box. 'Warned by an oracle that his grandson would kill him, Acrisius had taken his daughter Danaë and her babe, Perseus, to the sea-shore and put them into a chest and thrust them out to sea, for the winds and the waves to carry them whithersoever they would.

'The north-west wind blew freshly out of the blue mountains, and down the pleasant Vale of Argos, and away out to sea. And away and out to sea before it floated the mother and her babe, while all who watched them wept, save that cruel father, King Acrisius.

'So they floated on and on, and the chest danced up and down upon the billows, and the baby slept upon its mother's breast: the poor mother could not sleep, but watched and wept, and she sang to her baby as they floated.

'And they passed the last blue headland, and they were in the open sea; and there was nothing around them but waves, and the sky, and the wind. But the waves were gentle, and the sky was clear, and the breeze was tender and low.

'So a night passed, and a day, and a long day it was for Danaë; and another night and day beside, till Danaë was faint from thirst and weeping; and yet no land appeared. They went on in their little wooden chest. And the babe slept quietly; and at last poor Danaë drooped her head and fell asleep with her cheek against the babe's.

'She was awakened suddenly for the chest was jarring and grinding, and the air was full of sound. She looked up, and over her head were mighty cliffs, all red in the setting sun, and around her rocks and breakers, and flying flakes of foam. She clasped her hands together, and shrieked aloud for help. And when she cried, help met her...'

Here Mary paused, for here the similarity of the legend and her reality finished. She had cried for help but no man or ship had come. Ah Sam did not understand but he listened as Mary sped through the rest of the legend. She was excited; perhaps by relating the story she would find the key for now.

148

'Danaë and Perseus were lifted out of the chest by a king's brother and taken to the island of Seriphus. Perseus grew up and, after many adventures, wearing winged sandals — a present from the gods — he ran through empty air and along the sky. He slayed Gorgon and became a hero. Later he and his beautiful wife, Andromeda, reigned over Argos.'

Mary smiled, she always loved this part of the story. 'And when they died, the Ancients say, Athené took them up into the sky and there on starlight nights you may see them shining still — Perseus with the Gorgon's head and fair Andromeda beside him, spreading her long white arms across the heaven. All night long they shine, for a beacon to wandering sailors: but all day they feast with the gods, on the still blue peaks of Olympus.'

Instead of dreading the approach of darkness that long Monday, Mary longed for it. She could hardly wait to see the star Perseus in the Milky Way. Her urge to see the star was intense — the need to have a link, tenuous though it may appear, with something beyond the horror of being in the smelly tank. Sunset brought immense anticipation and she started turning her face towards the heavens, beyond the unimaginable. At last it was dark; one by one the stars shone down.

No, no. Not that one. Her eyes swivelled across the sky, searching. Not that one. But Perseus should be there, she was sure that Perseus was visible in the tropics in the southern hemisphere during the spring. After the equinox the star slipped down for a few months. But it was not there. Tears streamed down Mary's face. She kept looking up into the flat confusion of stars. At last, at about 9 o'clock, first she saw the shape of Andromeda and then Perseus appearing above the horizon, both very low in the eastern sky. She clasped her hands in joy. It was an omen; it certainly augured something, but what? If at the very time that she was re-enacting Perseus's first flight his stars should make one of their rare appearances above her, surely...

She sat there, stiff and uncomfortable, trying not to lick her lips; the delicious salty sea spray on them would only make her more thirsty. The Constellation Crux — the great Southern Cross — could not be seen because in October and November it is not visible anywhere north of Brisbane. That was another omen, Mary was sure.

The Southern Cross had been a disappointment when Mary had first seen it from the deck of the *City of Agra* five years earlier. The four main stars of the Southern Cross, although a favourite theme of travellers and poets, and used by sailors to navigate by, is a dull group. Dante, who had used the four stars to symbolize the four moral virtues — justice, prudence, temperance and fortitude — had described them as bright, but they were not, Mary thought. She was suddenly giddy; she felt herself revolving as ever towards the east, faster, faster. She heard the earth whizz.

From the time the sun rose until it sank Mary's and Ah Sam's eyes scanned the sea, hoping, hoping that they would see another ship. She prayed, 'Please God. We have been preserved so long. We shall be left to perish.' And when they weren't searching the sea, they looked to the sky eagerly for signs of rain. Day after day, the sun rose into a clear sky only to sink again into the same cloudless horizon.

Mary covered up the little tin of water so that it would not evaporate. Their throats were parched but she would only allow them just enough water to wet their lips when thirst was unbearable. She told Ah Sam that on no condition was he to drink the sea-water for sailors said that madness and death followed.

Mary's desire to retreat, to go back so she would live under a familiar galaxy, was strong. When she started writing her diary again that Wednesday she even tried to make time regress. As soon as today is yesterday it is gone; squashed into the past which becomes nothing but a few brain cells, memories to feed dreams. The past is within us; and so is time. But, thought Mary, the sun shines earlier on Australia than it does in England, ten hours earlier, so today here is tomorrow there.

Time, she thought, that is measured by clocks is a false thing, for clocks are a recent mechanical way of dividing the span it takes for the earth to turn on its axis. The day is true but hours and years are man-made. Only since 1200 has time been man-made and turned something as visible as the trees and the flowers into an abstract concept. 'Six o'clock' or 'ten o'clock' is a numerical expression of the distance the earth has travelled around the sun. Although geared to the earth's rotation, a clock is a modern substitute for reading the heavenly bodies during the earth's spin to gauge how long it will take before it completes a full revolution around the sun.

The 31st December, New Year's Eve, celebrates the earth's safe arrival to the position it had started its journey from; New Year's Day celebrates the beginning of yet another journey. Each race starts the journey when the earth is at a different position — there is the Chinese starting point, the Moslem beginning, the Christian beginning...

Everything that moves — water, grass or woman — is in rhythm with celestial movement in this sun-centred universe. Time is within us. The sea with its tides is the earth's time; day after day Mary felt the moon sending the water leaping high on the beaches and pulling it away again. Up and down they went.

But for Mary time had slipped back. When on the Wednesday she resumed her comforting habit of writing daily in her journal, for each entry she put 'September'. It was October.

Despairing and alone she wrote:

Left Lizard Island September 2nd, 1881 (Sunday afternoon) in tank or pot in which *bêche-de-mer* is boiled. Got about three miles or four from the Lizards.

150

September 4. Made for the sand bank off the Lizards but could not reach it. Got on a reef all day on the look-out for a boat, but saw none.
September 6. Very calm morning. Able to pull the tank up to an island with three small mountains on it. Ah Sam went ashore to try and get water as ours was done. There were natives camped there so we were afraid to go far away. We had to wait return of tide. Anchored under the mangroves, got on the reef. Very calm.

As she wrote in her diary on 7 October there appeared in the distance a dark form sliding slowly towards her. And then she recognized its red and white funnel and the red duster — it was a British ship. On the steamer came, nearer and nearer, her funnel seen clearly against the sky. Mary's heart beat anxiously. Would a rowing boat be lowered and sent to pick them up?

'Ahoy, Ahoy', she yelled until her voice was exhausted. She

waited. She hoisted the baby's large white shawl so it fluttered like a flag. I shall be left alone, this is my only hope, she thought as her voice rose again. 'Ahoy! Ship Ahoy!'

'We're seen. We're seen, yes we are seen!' she exclaimed to Ah Sam. But the ship sailed on.

September 7. Made for an island four or five miles from the one spoken of yesterday. Ashore, but could not find any water. Cooked some rice and clam-fish. Moderate S.E. breeze. Stayed here all night. Saw a steamer bound north. Hoisted Ferrier's white and pink wrap but did not answer us.

September 8. Changed the anchorage of the boat as the wind was freshening. Went down to a kind of little lake on the same island (this done last night). Remained here all day looking out for a boat; did not see any. Very cold night; blowing very hard. No water.

Vain was the search for water. Ah Sam and Mary surveyed every inch of the islet, not a sign of a spring could be discovered. Not only weeks, but months, years, might go by before any vessel passed close enough to see them. They had neither the means nor the energy to make a sensational signal. Ah Sam suggested building a hut to shelter them from the heat of the day, the chill of the night and the wet season when it came. But they had no strength. Ah Sam managed to dig a hole, though, with three trenches leading into it, to collect any rain water that came.

'Water, water, water', she muttered. 'I am just one of the thousands and thousands of people and animals from Europe who live in Australia waiting with open mouth, waiting for the rain.' The animals and vegetation that were native to this dry continent had adapted themselves to the dryness and the unreliable rainfall. The koala bear never drank, it got enough water from gum leaves.

Mary thought of Nanhellon, of East Wheal Rose where the men died as a result of excessive rain. Just a drop of it now. She thought of the fig tree that flourished even during dry spells when everything withered. She wished that she had some of its mysterious strength. She saw the church of St Newlyna. Ah Sam saw the Great Pagoda, rising beautiful and massive with gilded pinnacles. They slept. At dawn a bird came down and perched on the branch of the mangrove tree close to Mary. It had a yellow breast and sang a sweet song. The bird waited until she woke and then flew up and away on the wings she needed.

September 9. Brought the tank ashore as far as possible with this morning's tide. Made camp all day under the trees. Blowing very hard. No water. Gave Ferrier a dip in the sea; he is showing symptoms of thirst, and I took a dip myself. Ah Sam and self very parched with thirst. Ferrier showing symptoms.

September 10. Ferrier very bad with inflammation; very much alarmed. No fresh water, and no more milk, but condensed. Self very weak; really thought I would have died last night (Sunday).

September 11. Still all alive. Ferrier much better this morning. Self feel-

153

ing very weak. I think it will rain today, clouds very heavy, wind not quite so hard. No rain. Morning fine weather. Ah Sam preparing to die. Have not seen him since 9. Ferrier more cheerful. Self not feeling at all well. Have not seen any boat of any description. No water. Near dead with thirst.

Here the pencil stopped — forever. The sensation of thirst was so great that she wet her mouth with salt water to try to allay the dry, hot condition of her palate and tongue. Tighter and tighter she gripped the baby to her breast. Her delirium was now accompanied by visual illusions. She was not sure exactly when the baby died, she clung on to him delirious. If tears could quench thirst — but a parched and swollen throat cannot swallow. The last remaining provisions were left untouched.

Mary looked to the sky, waiting for the rain. She drew a deep breath of exhaustion. She slept. It was the loveliest sleep that she ever had — deep and dreamless. She clung to the baby. She saw the ship coming towards her, the white canvas shining in the moonlight; she saw the green, fertile landscape of Cornwall... the bluebells were there near the church of St Newlyna. And the branches of the fig tree were reaching out to entwine her, to grasp her, lift her up and

take her away from the snaggy mangroves. Her legs and arms went limp.

Two days later the sky filled with dark clouds and it rained so heavily that the bodies of Mary and the baby were drenched in a torrent of water.

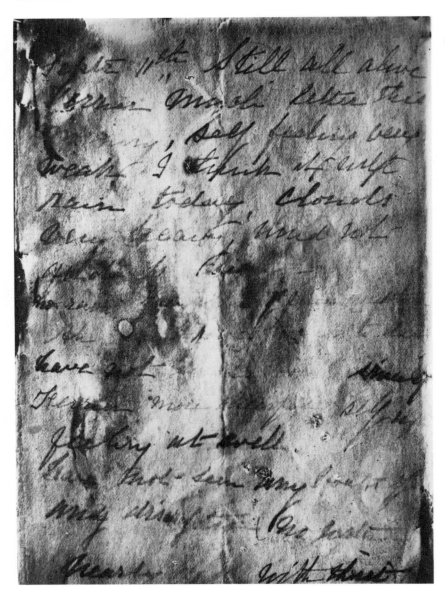

Chapter Eighteen

The Aborigines Regain their Island

Fires were an integral part of Aboriginal culture. They were kept burning during the night and when easy fuel ran out even their huts, built only for brief occupation, were broken up and burnt. A dwelling was not durable, not to be possessed and owned. It only took a few hours to build a shelter — by stripping a few sheets of bark off the nearest trees and propping them up with saplings. The Aborigines were nomads and had no concept of a home, no need for a place in which the civilized hide from the world and act out trifling personal rituals and habits. For Aborigines a roof was only for shelter; a thing that would be replaced. Their security was not within permanent walls on a small plot; it was within vast communal territories known as ancestral lands.

The Aborigines did not have the instinct to surround themselves with objects and personal possessions. Possessions were not for the benefit of the individual but for the benefit of the group; 'my' means 'our'. They did not understand why a white man kept working and exhausting himself beyond the point of filling his belly, just to buy things to look at or sit on, or show-off; working to own something.

The Aborigines knew that certain birds would always return to their nests even if they had gone great distances from them — just as ants and bees always returned to their hives. But Aborigines, unfettered with needs for individual plots or homes, could not feel how distressed Mary would have been when they pulled things out of her granite cottage, turning the neat domestic order which had cost such effort, into disorder. Order and tidiness had been so important; she could always lay her hands on the milk-pan or the blue stockings, even in the dark.

The emu-feather dandy pulled down the biscuit tins and gobbled up the shortbread before the tribal men ran in. Grabbing and wrecking was swift. Like rape. They even smashed her sewing machine; sharp pieces of metal made good spears. Papers, clothes, photographs and books were taken or scattered. The cover was ripped off *David Copperfield* Volume II. The wind picked up the loose pages and scattered them further along the beach and into the sea. All her life was nothing.

When the tribal feast and sacking were over the men climbed into their canoes and went back across the sea.

The birds waited on the fourth branch of the Casuarina tree as they always did for Mary and pecked at the dry drinking bowl until the sky filled with dark clouds and it rained so heavily that the bowl overflowed. Again the island was uninhabited as it had been for thousands of years; again the lizards reigned supreme. The hush and stillness came back. Ah Leong's garden was overgrown with weeds. Everything grows so quickly in the tropics.

Captain Watson was away longer than planned. He slept lightly under the leaking canvas tent and dreamt deeply... A 'cockatoo' was patrolling outside the two-up school behind the Cooktown wharves, ready to whistle a warning if the cops came. Bob took Mary's hand and led her into a grubby, badly ventilated room. The walls were padded up with sugar bags to deaden the sound of the excited voices. A tall heavy man with a long black beard without a collar studded into his shirt stood in the middle of the room. He was the spinner. Around him clustered an assortment of men from all classes and countries. Bets and the kip were handed to the spinner. Slowly the spinner took the two copper pennies, adjusted them according to some predetermined system, then tossed them dexterously into the air. A fair toss! All eyes and heads rose and fell with the coins. Swiftly the coins came down, falling noiselessly on sugar bags. After an eager peering at the upturned coins — heads or tails, Queen Victoria or the kangaroo — the result was announced in a loud whisper. Winnings were paid over. But Captain Watson didn't win. He lost — everything.

The squawking and noise of the thousands of Torres Strait pigeons had woken him out of his dream. Every morning they flew out of the trees towards the mainland and returned at dusk. It was just after dawn at the end of October. Captain Watson had been fishing in the reefs around Night Island for two months now. It was a lengthy time to leave Mary alone but the Night Island cottage had been started, the smoke-house was completed and they wanted to get some money in before the weather changed to the monsoon. Life, he thought, in Australia is a gamble. Australia is just a giant green baize table, the biggest gaming table in the world. You stake everything against the weather, against chance. Captain Watson was having another go, throwing another dice, having another round, placing another bet.

Like the tens of thousands of English, Irish, Cornish and Scots who sailed to North Queensland in the 1860s and 1870s Captain Watson had come to Australia with hope, hope of dreams. He had given up certainty in the old world, for the uncertain vision of wealth that he hoped to find in his new land. Migration was a way of disowning the past. Once a pioneer arrived in the north, though, once on the hot dusty earth, the drudgery needed just to keep dirt-free, fed and watered left a man exhausted. Hope kept them going. Hope of finding gold; hope of living like a squire on vast acres; hope of dreams. A place where dreams would become reality.

After a few months of not knowing where the next meal or gulp of water was coming from, or whether the swarms of mosquitoes were malaria-carriers, or whether a snake was in the bed roll or whether the rustle in the bushes was those 'damn blacks' silently tracking with spears to hurl through the closest chest, gradually the hope gave away to a dependence on 'if'. If it rains; if I get there first; if the horse gets there first. I could be content if...

Reward in Queensland was not for individual merit; it was luck. Whereas in England the principle of a fair day's work for a fair day's pay had become accepted, here it was different; a man controlled his own destiny not by hard work, but with hope. Digging two feet away from another bloke and hitting gold; or digging three feet away from another digger who gets the gold while all you get is a 'duffer'; land grants on profitable soil, or arid soil; government

Men arrived full of hope

favours; town planning granted on farm lands; speculations; shares; rain. If only. You can work or dig day and night for years and lose everything because the clouds don't bring rain. The droughts last for years and a farmer has to watch his sheep and cattle — his living cash — slowly die. He has failed; the plans of a lifetime have become illusions.

Towns in Australia often have a Hope Street but they seldom have a Luck Street or an If Street, although the word 'if' and the phrase 'if only' are frequently used. An Australian will bet on anything — horses, cards, dice or lottery. Australia is a country where destiny is unfair every day to someone; so much is chance. So much is If. This makes the place a true democracy — a country where everyone has a chance, to win or to suffer.

This made it all a frightful beginning for a new country, especially for the middle classes, or aspiring workers. They could not control their lives; they could not insure against hunger by work, industry and thrift. Men at the top often got there just by luck, after taking a few chances.

The uncertainty of this existence pushed everyone into the safety of dull suburbs as soon as they could fence off the threats with wooden palings; a place where they could nestle. All this came with secure jobs and wage packets — wages and money for merit — where life and money could be controlled. A place with a brick church where even God could be controlled, his benevolence purchased by placing money in the brass plate and performing good deeds.

Like many Queenslanders, Captain Watson did not win; things almost worked out, but not quite. Despite his marriage, migration and travel had not given happiness to him; less, perhaps, than his homeland, Scotland, might have supplied. Too much wandering in pleasant by-paths — the road was never clear before him. Captain Watson was just one of the million of the great migration; one of the thousands who had followed Mr Micawber to Australia but not grasped the same success as the Charles Dickens hero. Captain Watson had brought his problems with him as if they were tangible objects packed in his trunk. Everywhere he went the same familiar old sins had found room; evil tempts in all places. Parted from a town, a country and traditions which his family had sprung from for generations, he had no real anchor in Queensland. And he was used to one.

Marriage, he realized, was a short tether. He loved Mary but he was no longer mobile; he could no longer rush where a better chance might await. His home could no longer simply be under his hat. Like many emigrants Captain Watson never adapted to his new land and yet he no longer belonged to his homeland. He could join in with the kilts and bagpipes, but he could not go forward. He belonged nowhere; he had grown into a typical emigrant, almost an outsider. Like so many travellers he would have found more contentment by

staying still and looking gently inwards than by traversing the earth, searching and searching. A new environment seldom makes a difference to the heart.

Captain Watson had become a man whose life was full of partings, new instant friendships, and friendships quickly forgotten. As Henry Lawson observed, 'The mateship born in barren lands, Of toil and thirst and danger'. Going abroad had seemed such a good idea to Captain Watson. He had been so lured by the idea of a fresh start. Ferrier's life, perhaps, would be better. It was usually the progeny of emigrants, through progressive adaptation to the environment, who reaped the benefits of migration. Captain Watson thought of Ferrier. Oh, how he longed to say, 'And so I am going home, home to my own people'.

Captain Watson did not know he was free again; did not know that his wife and child were already dead.

SAD TIDINGS
(Extract Cooktown "Courier," October, 1881.)

Some six weeks ago, Mr. P.C. Fuller and Captain R.F. Watson, both well-known in Cooktown, who had been residing for some months on one of the Lizard Islands, left for Knight [sic] Island a little over 200 miles distance north, with the view of forming a fishing station, leaving Mrs. Watson and her baby and two Chinamen in charge of the station. Captain Frier reported after his arrival at Cooktown on Wednesday, the 19th October, 1881, that when he passed the Lizard Island on Monday evening, the 17th October, 1881, bush fires were numerous, and on nearing the land he made signals, but received no answer, and observing that the door of the hut was open, with two blackfellows about the place, he concluded the station had been broken up, and sailed on his course for Cooktown. On Thursday, the 20th October, 1881, the Neptune, cutter, in charge of some Chinamen, who returned from searching for their vessel in that locality, saw eight or ten native canoes hauled up on the beach, and about forty blacks on the Lizard Island, where a bush fire was raging. They reported the case to Mr. Fahey, Sub-Collector of Customs, Cooktown, who, with his usual promptitude, communicated at once with Inspector Fitzgerald, who consented to allow a police officer with five troopers to accompany him to the Lizard Island. Arrangements were made to leave, but Leut. Izatt, of H.M.S. Conflict, hearing of the affair, offered to convey the party, which left on the 21st October, 1881, in the Conflict. Mr. Fahey takes with him one of the Customs boatmen, as well as the police, and expects to return on Sunday, the 23rd October, 1881. In the meantime further intelligence is awaited in Cooktown with much anxiety.

Mary (Queensland Museum)

Chapter Nineteen

The Discovery

They found her on 16 January the day before her twenty-second birthday. Mrs Watson was right; she had known that she and Ah Sam would be picked up by a passing boat. Walking across Howick No. 5 Island, the mate from the *Kate Kearney* saw a skeleton: 'It was covered with a quilt up to the ribs. The skull rested on a small Chinese pillow. Between the skull and the pillow was some human hair attached to which was tape forming a Chinese tail...' An unloaded snider rifle, some cartridges and a sheath knife lay beside him.

Amongst the snaggy branches of the mangrove trees more human hair hung over the rim of a four-foot square iron tank. The monsoonal rain had filled the tank so the mate had to perforate the sides and bottom with an axe to let the water drain out. He saw the fully clothed skeleton of Mrs Watson with a baby embraced by her right arm at her breast. Her big hand gripped the tiny finger bones.

Mrs Watson's legs lay across the rusty tank beside a loaded revolver, fully cocked, and a camphorwood box. 'I opened the box and took out first a book and a pencil. On the former I saw "Lizard Island"...'

Captain Watson always thought of her, his lovely bride. He went to get her two days after they had found her. He had known for the sixteen weeks of searching that he would be with her again: to touch her, even if just to say 'goodbye' and to say he was sorry.

The Water Police Magistrate, Mr B. Fahey, said that the Coroner's Court would be held on board H.M.S. *Spitfire* after they had picked up the bodies. At Cooktown crowds had watched them board the ship at the wharf opposite French Charley's — there was the Clerk of the Court, together with Inspector Fitzgerald, Mr

162

The Courthouse, Cooktown (John Oxley Library)

Scott, who had found the bodies in the tank, and Captain Watson.

After a day at sea H.M.S. *Spitfire* arrived at Howick No. 5 Island. A rowing boat took the party across the lagoon and then Mr Scott led them single file through the scrub to the mangrove swamps near the little lake, the saltwater lake which had been a mirage of drinkable liquid and had lured Mary to land.

The tank was covered with a sheet of galvanized iron. Mr Scott explained that he had put it on to protect the remains from the sun and the rain. But it was not really to save the little that was left of her, it was because he was embarrassed by death. He had been embarrassed by her skeleton, although it was partly clothed. And now Mr Scott was more self-conscious when he took off the iron sheet to expose the corpses lying in the tank; he looked at Captain Watson to see if he was disturbed at other men seeing his wife so naked.

Captain Watson touched the tank, the tool which had for so many years killed and boiled the *bêche-de-mer* to earn his livelihood, and which had now killed Mary, the only person he had ever admitted to loving. Outside his ears complete silence echoed — the shrill of cicadas was too familiar to hear. But inside his head he spoke to her. Slowly he lent forward and touched the white bones of her hand, that hand which had so often reached out for his. Her brown eyes, her skin and her flesh had gone, but she was with him again. He was not alone anymore. He picked her up and clung to her, put his arms

163

around that tiny waist still encircled with a brown belt, but as always the baby was between them. Ferrier was still at her breast.

When he picked her up he could not bring himself to touch her mouth, now just jaws and teeth. He kissed her forehead instead; as he did so encompassing love and resentment came over him. He had always, always known it would not last, that she would not stay with him. That had been the trouble. She had needed the security he gave her, but had wanted to be free. He had always known that she would leave him; go away and leave him. He had never trusted her; he felt she had never really loved him, that what she said was love was just need. When they had been happy he had always had the fear that it would not last. He pulled the skeleton closer to him as he lent into the tank.

He saw the light of her brown eyes shining on him; heard the blurred tone of her voice. Fate had parted them before time could destroy their relationship, before it had time to chill. Even when they had sat on the hard smooth sand in their bay at Lizard Island and their moods had blended together into bliss, he had always been looking for signs that it would not last; always waiting for her superior tongue. Or boredom. Or restlessness. But now it was all right. He was with her and it was all over but it was all right. He escaped into a state of delirium. He saw the green, fertile landscape of Cornwall and Mary was walking across a grassy headland above a beach, and she was reaching over to pick the daffodils...

It was dusk and night falls quickly in the tropics, so they led him back to the rowing boat, Inspector Fitzgerald took one arm, Mr Scott the other. It was all over now.

A.

Evidence taken before me: B. FAHEY, W.P.M., into the circumstances attending the death and identification of the bodies of MARY BEATRICE PHILLIPS WATSON: GEORGE FERRIER WATSON: and AH SAM.

WILLIAM HENRY SCOTT, being duly sworn states: I remember the 18th instant. I believe it was last Wednesday. I was on that day passing in the vessel called the Kate Kearney through the Howick group of islands. I am mate of that vessel. On that day I ordered some of the black boys on board that vessel to land on Number 5, Howick, and cook some fish for themselves, caught by means of lines as the vessel was sailing.

About 4 o'clock in the afternoon two of the black boys returned to the vessel and reported that they discovered some human remains. I then landed on the island and saw from 15 to 20 yards (on the island) above high-water mark, the skeleton of a human being, showing signs of recent decomposition. It was covered with a quilt up to the ribs. The skull rested on a small Chinese pillow. Between the skull and the pillow was some human hair attached to which was tape forming a Chinese tail or queue. I at once concluded the remains were those of a Chinaman. I saw those remains this morning and assisted to place them in a coffin brought from Cooktown.

B.

BY INSPECTOR FITZGERALD: I recognize this paper [paper produced] as an agreement between Messrs. Fuller and Watson and Ah Sam. I know the document to have been picked up in the vicinity of the Chinese remains this morning by your trooper. I saw the trooper hand it to you and pointed out to you where he got it. I saw the box used as a pillow by the Chinaman. I forced the top off, and found in it two sticks of tobacco, a stone for sharpening a razor, and two Chinese books — and alongside him were a snider, not loaded, and a sheath knife, also some cartridges.

Sgd. William Henry Scott.

Taken and sworn before me, this 24th day of January, 1882
on board H.M. Ship Spitfire
Sgd. B. Fahey, W.P.M.

C.

EXAMINATION OF WILLIAM HENRY SCOTT continued: I also saw the lower portion of an iron tank. I examined it. It lay just at high-water mark on the S.W. side of the island almost concealed from observation in the mangroves. I saw in the tank what I took to be the body of a woman, nearly covered with fresh water, in the last stage of decomposition and clad. I perforated with an axe the bottom of the tank, also the sides by a snider bullet to allow the water to escape and then recognized the skeleton of a child on the woman's breast encompassed by her arm. A loaded revolver by her side, full-cocked, and a camphorwood box.

I opened the box and took out first a book and pencil. On the former I saw written 'Lizard Island.' I then at once concluded the remains to be those of Mrs. Watson and her child. I handed the book to Capt. Bremner. I subsequently read it by the aid of a magnifying glass and found it to be a diary kept by Mrs. Watson from the date she left Lizard Island. I unpacked the chest, found baby's clothes and woman's clothing and jewellery, including watch, rings and money, comprised of notes, silver and gold amounting to about three pounds (£3). I also found two tins of sardines, one tin of patent goat's milk and a package of matches. All of the clothing fit to be taken, jewellery and money I kept in my own possession until delivered to Mr. Watson in Cooktown. Also I took on the revolver. I have frequently been on Number 5 Howick at all seasons of the year and never saw fresh water there — there are no springs on the island. I saw evidence of the blacks on the island within the last month where they had been cooking turtles on the N.W. end of it. I removed the tank above high-water mark, assisted by the ship's crew and covered it with galvanized iron taken from the ship.

D.

BY INSPECTOR FITZGERALD: I found the articles that had been used for a signal and the staff. The former rolled up, pinned together and packed away in the box. I saw where a fire had been made on the beach. In the tank, also there was a saw, hammer, saucepan and an umbrella — and the box.

Sgd. William Henry Scott.

Taken and sworn before me, this 24th day of January, 1882,
on board H.M. Ship Spitfire
Sgd. B. Fahey, W.P.M.

ROBERT WATSON being duly sworn, states: I am a *bêche-de-mer* fisher residing at present in Cooktown and belong to the firm of Fuller and Watson. I have recently resided at Lizard Island and first went to reside there in 1879. I built on Lizard Island a dwelling, smoke and storehouse, and cultivated a small portion of the island.

I was married on the 30th May, 1880 to Mary Beatrice Phillips Oxenham (*sic*). Subsequent to our marriage we resided on the Lizard Island, and since. In March last year (1881) my wife went to reside in Cooktown pending her accouchement and returned to the island about the end of June last, being then the mother of a male child born on the 3rd June.

On the 1st September, I left with my partner Fuller, taking our boats to fish northward on a six-weeks' cruise.

About the end of October while fishing at Restoration Island, I was informed that the Aborigines from the mainland had attacked the island and that my wife, child and two Chinamen who were left on the Lizard Island in charge were missing, and my houses sacked and property all destroyed. Upon my immediate return to Lizard this report was confirmed by personal observation. Since the 7th November last I have been untiring in my search for traces of my wife and child, assisted by the police and Harbour authorities and others, amongst the islands and coast land between Cooktown and Cape Melville.

From information I received I visited No. 5 Island Howick Group this morning in the Government Schooner Spitfire accompanied by Harbour-master Fahey and the Inspector of Police. On this island I found the remains of my wife and child.

I recognized the body of my wife, although in a state of decomposition, by her clothing, a leather belt she wore round her waist and her hair. I also produce a ring — I remember its being made by a Chinaman in Cooktown and subsequently placed by me on the third finger of her left hand on the occasion of our marriage. The ring I now produce I took off her finger this morning and recognized it as the one placed by me on her finger on the occasion of our marriage.

I also identify a revolver found in the vicinity of the body as the one left by me on Lizard Island in the beginning of September last. A box containing clothing, jewellery and two (£1) one pound notes, half sovereign and silver, also her diary, I identify as our property.

The diary in which is recorded in pencil the circumstances attending my wife's departure from Lizard Island, I recognize as her handwriting. I recognize the remains of the child by its clothing found on it and in the vicinity. The child's name was Thomas Ferrier Watson.

I also recognize portion of an iron tank in which I found the bodies of my wife and child on No. 5 Howick, as that I used for a *bêche-de-mer* boiler on Lizard Island — also two paddles which I picked up near the boiler and identified.

I also saw the remains of a Chinaman lately in my employ named Ah Sam. I saw them on the island in the vicinity of my wife and child. I recognize them to be those of the Chinaman from the peculiarity of his hair, the clothing and contents of his box — and identify a rifle found alongside the body as one left by me with my wife on Lizard Island. I believe that my wife, child and the Chinaman Ah Sam, died from thirst.

I make this statement from circumstances related by my wife in her diary which records I recognize as her handwriting.

Sgd. Robert Watson.

Taken and sworn before me on board Government Schooner Spitfire this 24th day of January, 1882.
Sgd. B. Fahey, W.P.M.

167

Chapter Twenty

The Battle Lost

Always he was with her, his lovely bride.

The flags of the vessels in port and on the flagstaffs were at half-mast all day. The bodies were removed from the police station on the previous evening by Messrs Clunn & Sons, and placed in the Town Hall. They dressed her in white — someone had mended her torn wedding dress. Then they arranged her long brown hair — instead of a skeleton she was an angel.

The baby was wrapped in a lace shawl and placed under her right arm, that safe place where he had spent most of his life of nineteen weeks. Captain Watson was in his black suit already so he would not have to go back to the West Coast Hotel and change before the funeral. They said he could sit there beside the coffin until the lid was sealed late on Sunday morning. They were still getting the flowers ready; it was difficult to find enough with all the heavy rain.

The coffin was on the carpet so he had to kneel. The ladies whispered that he was 'in a state'. Captain Watson suffered anguish for leaving Mary on Lizard Island, but was angry with her for dying. He had always been nervous that she would leave him. Now she had. Now he had returned to those bleak days of being alone; but now he had known love he would be doubly alone, with no one to care, no one to come home to, no one to try and please, no one to react. People in Cooktown were friendly, yes, but he knew it was not because of popularity, he had never been popular, it was because they were cashing in on his grief. And when they would say, 'So young, only twenty-one', he was sure they were looking at his wrinkled face and browning hands and thinking, 'She was a bit young for him; he must have been twice her age'. He crumpled up, sobbing his heart out.

He had loved her so much. Better she had deserted him by dying than by retreating from him with permanent physical coldness, as when she would not look up but would reply to him with a murmur, 'Oh, wait till I finish this chapter. I must finish this chapter', and continue reading and ignoring him. Even when he made a movement, a mute appeal, she would read on. She would walk miles just to borrow a tatty, old coverless book. So often she had lived in a world of the mind. Tears came again and he looked away.

The church ladies had gone to butter the scones for refreshments after the burial. At last Captain Watson was alone with her. Again he slowly lent forward and touched the white bones of her hands, those hands which had so often reached out for his. He wanted to pick her up, one last time. But the ladies from the church had requested him not to disturb her, 'We've gone to such a lot of trouble to get her looking nice. Doesn't the necklace and the ring make all the difference?'

Again he felt her soft hair on his face and in his eyes. Bliss ran through him as his hand lay over hers. But then the ladies came back. They wouldn't leave him alone, all these people. Not for them to miss the obscure sensation that goes with disaster. Captain Watson was not used to sharing things and now he was sharing sorrow. Instead of a simple interment the funeral had become an event. So hungry were the Cooktowners for community ritual that Mrs Watson's tragedy had given them something in common apart from the ambition to make money or find gold.

In the eight years that Cooktown had taken to grow out of the bush it had attracted people from everywhere; there were too many groups with too many backgrounds and no cohesiveness. Everyone came from somewhere else. And being so new it had no comforting landmarks, no traditions, no relics from the past. Everything had just happened, nothing had evolved. The funeral of Mrs Watson was the largest funeral ever held in North Queensland — and for Cooktown it was the biggest of social occasions.

The church bells of St Joseph's and St Mary's started their sonorous tollings at 1.30 p.m. The streets were sombre; the drums of the Fire Brigade Band were muffled and covered with black crepe. For two nights they had been rehearsing the Dead March from *Saul* and Pleyel's 'German Hymn', covering Cooktown in a cloak of sadness.

The church was too small. At 2 p.m. the Church of England vicar, the Reverend Mr Hosken, who had performed Mary's wedding ceremony twenty months earlier, read the first prayers of the burial service to the 650 townsfolk and bushmen who had crowded into the hall and jammed along the pavement and road outside under the awnings and verandahs. Despite the heat, many mourners were in outfits of black serge, black bombazine or lustreless alpaca, bonnets of black crepe, black gloves; some gentlemen just wore a black band on the left arm and on the hat. The Chinese wore both black and their traditional mourning colour of white.

169

Percy Fuller and Bob Hartley joined Captain Watson to represent the family. No one from Mary's family came to the funeral. Captain Watson had sent a telegraph message to Rockhampton. Papa broke down. He really wasn't in a state to travel the 800 miles north to Cooktown. Mamma thought it would be too much for him to see his favourite daughter buried. Papa had so wanted to go and say goodbye to his girl.

Oh, but they came from everywhere else. Usually on that last frontier of the north every man was out for himself: the line between living and dying was thin. Failure meant no meat, no bread, no tea, no water, no rum. Death. Now Mary spread her long white arms around these floating disunited strugglers for the celebration of death. It was Mary's angel who inspired the giant inscription painted in clear letters on a banner across the stage: 'One is All', a distortion of the Cornish motto, 'One and All'.

'All is One' or 'One is All'? Behind the vicar, sixty-seven schoolchildren in crisp uniforms guarded the two coffins draped in black. On Mary's a smaller banner of this distorted Cornish motto 'One is All' was centred on a floral wreath. A fine floral cross had been artistically prepared by Mr J.C. Street. The bandsmen were on one side of the hall with their sheet music; the Fire Brigade on the other; the Good Templars and the Cooktowners who had got there early enough to get a place were in the centre.

A thousand voices were raised to sing the Twenty-third Psalm:

> The Lord is my shepherd; I shall not want. He maketh me to lie down in green pastures: he leadeth me beside the still waters. He restoreth my soul: he leadeth me in the paths of righteousness for his name's sake. Yea, though I walk through the valley of the shadow of death, I will fear no evil: for thou art with me; thy rod and thy staff they comfort me. Thou preparest a table before me in the presence of mine enemies: thou anointest my head with oil; my cup runneth over...

There were emotional scenes; some members of the congregation sobbed, others openly wept. It was so hot that the blokes from the bush were wiping the sweat off their foreheads with their rolled up sleeves. No opera chorus, no trained choir, could ever have sung more out of tune with more fervour or feeling than the mourners that Sabbath. With heavy hearts they prayed to God, and with voices loud they sang. On they went, hymn after prayer, prayer after psalm, louder and heartier with every beat of the brass band. Mrs Watson's death symbolized the deaths of all the immigrants who had died in that primeval battle against nature. Out there, beyond, hundreds were dying or would die.

The vicar read the last page in the bible as the main lesson: Revelations, Chapter 22:

> And he shewed me a pure river of water of life, clear as crystal, proceeding out of the throne of God...

For without are dogs, and sorcerers, and whoremongers, and murderers, and idolaters, and whatsoever...

And the Spirit and the bride say, Come. And let him that heareth say, Come. And let him that is athirst come. And whosoever will, let him take the water of life freely...

The Fire Brigade, headed by the band with their muffled drums, marched at the head of the long procession 'to accompany the corpse on its last journey'. The chief mourners headed by Captain Watson, Mr Fuller, Monsieur Bouel, Mr Hartley and Assistant Superintendent Emanuel of the Fire Brigade came after the hearse which was drawn by four black horses. On they followed in that great march with the booming brass band under the scorching sun: the Lord Mayor and Municipal Councillors, the Police Magistrate, the sub-collector of Customs, the Good Templars, schoolchildren — the Church of England then the convent children. The police were omitted from the programme — not as an intentional slight but by pure accident. They mustered well in private clothes and marched with the general public. The vehicles and horsemen followed. Keeping foot pace to the rolling beat of the drums they marched — Jew and Methodist, Greek and Lutheran, Catholic and Protestant. 'One is All', 'All is One', 'We are One'. Escapist and opportunist, rootless wanderer and Mr Almost-I-Am they marched: left, right, left, right, left, right, mourner and spectator, the butcher, the baker, the swag who had left his blanket and billy-can behind for the event. It took them thirty minutes to get down Charlotte Street and the Palmer Road. The bullock-waggons and drays had been banned for the afternoon and the roads swept of manure; the shops and houses were draped in black. 'Many ladies and children accompanied the procession, one who had known the deceased intimately following close to the hearse trying to hide her honourable grief behind the shade of a beautiful wreath, which she afterwards deposited in the grave', wrote the reporter for the Cooktown *Courier*.

At last the melancholy procession in silent awe arrived at the cemetery, that merciless dormitory of the dead. Few had either slabs, headstones or crosses; so many who died in those early days had no real friend, no family to buy or tend or care for them after their dying day. The Promised Land on the edge of the world had a soil too arid to nourish all the emigrants.

But on 29 January 1882, the diverse group of new settlers for once felt they belonged. They stood around the grave. The sods of earth — damp from the monsoonal rain — had been piled around the newly dug grave. It was the same size as a regulation English grave — six feet deep, six feet long and three feet wide.

The vicar said a few words from St Peter: 'For all flesh is of grass, and all the glory of man as the flower of grass. The grass withereth, and the flower falleth away...'

More words were said, more amens were chorused, more prayers offered, more people elbowed to get closer and have a look as the

Funeral procession, Cooktown

coffin containing Mary and the child was lowered. A solemn hush. A peace beyond all prayer as the spades shovelled the sods of earth upon the coffin, made of English elm so it would not rot for centuries. More eyes were red with tears. Voices were low. More brows were mopped; the effect of the formal mourning clothes in the calm hot mugginess of the wet season was showing. Blinding sunlight poured down on the dust.

It was 4 o'clock. Now the soil of that alien land lay gently on her.

The Assistant Superintendent of the Fire Brigade, Mr Emanuel, stepped up to the front: 'Comrades, let us before separating, uncover in honour of the memory of a brave woman'. Every hat was lifted, every bare head was reverently bowed. 'One is All', 'All is Nothing'. They stood there underneath England, at the bottom of the world. Was grief over now?

Ah Sam came next. 'The original programme was altered, and the lady's remains were first conveyed to the cemetery', reported the

172

Cooktown *Courier.* 'And this arrangement was probably an improvement, as the barbarous music of the Chinese band would have tried the nerves of horses and horsemen.' So after Mrs Watson had been committed to the earth the Fire Brigade, headed by the band, marched back to the Town Hall and headed the Chinese procession which accompanied the remains of Ah Sam in a typical Chinese coffin, a rough log hewn out like a primitive canoe and joined together again so that it looked as if they were carrying a log.

A Chinaman went ahead scattering pieces of paper. The Chinese band made desperate efforts to drown all sounds, and volleys of crackers were fired at very short intervals along the whole route. At the grave candles and charm-papers were burned, and the usual propitiatory libations were poured around the grave, then came another fusillade of crackers. Messrs Ti Chack and Kum Ching marshalled their countrymen. And they remembered the Emperor all those thousands of miles away in China, for he was high priest of all the people and 'vice-regent of heaven'.

At the end of the procession was a spring cart containing crackers, these being lighted and thrown down all along the road. The firemen having deposited the body in the grave, the Chinese made a fire on the brink of the grave and paid their accustomed marks of respect of the dead by bowing while crackers were freely thrown in all directions. At the gate they distributed brandy and Chinese drinks freely.

Except for one visit to salvage a few belongings and to search for the dogs, Captain Watson never returned to Lizard Island. He called and called the dogs but they were never found.

The last years of his life are unrecorded; all we know is that he had yet another fresh start and that severe back and chest pains forced him to give up marine life. He died on 22 October 1894 of

Chinese funeral

miners' phthisis, a side effect of pulmonary tuberculosis. The matron at Cooktown Hospital sent a telegraph message to his brother but it never found him.

No one gave Captain Watson a decent funeral, a headstone for his grave or even a slab to stop the weeds creeping across the mound over his wood coffin. As he was a Roman Catholic he was not buried beside his wife and baby. He is alone in the graveyard — out there lonely in the dark, the heat and the wet, the way he had spent most of his fifty-four years. The twenty months of marriage could not, it seems, change those patterns of solitude. Even today no one knows exactly where his grave is in the cemetery. After so many different resting places it would have been such a comfort if his last one had been beside her — quiet and still together. He was so weary when he died. So very weary. Vain was the effort to forget. He had missed her so much. Sometimes she spoke to him in dreams. Twenty-one, she always was, she never joined him in getting old and weary, not even in his mind. In those years before the weariness took over he could never hear the piano played without tears in his eyes — he always had to put his sleeve to his face and swallow hard. Once, just before he died, he had had to leave a pub because the pianist was playing Mary's Minute Waltz; he did not want the blokes to see him sobbing.

But she came to him in the end; she found him lying in his wretched den, lying on a miserable mattress, too weak to move, and with no one to help him. There was nothing to eat, not a farthing in his pocket. He had given up all in despair and laid himself down to die.

Epilogue

An enthusiastic punitive expedition dealt with various groups who were almost certainly the wrong Aborigines. The Mrs Watson tragedy was a unifying excuse; white settlers at last had a reason to vent their strong anti-black feelings. Emotions ran high. Continued raids by blacks on neighbouring properties and black tribal fights — occasionally even carried on in the streets of Cooktown itself — led to a formal curfew on Aborigines in 1885. They were banned from the town after dark.

In 1886, after a public subscription, a memorial was erected in the main street of Cooktown, just up from the fresh-water stream which had quenched Captain Cook and his crew in 1770. Today tourists see the baroque white marble column over a pedestal which originally had two public drinking taps. The inscription on the monument reads: 'In Memoriam, Mrs Watson, the heroine of Lizard Island, Cooktown, North Queensland, A.D. 1881', followed by the last stanza of a poem by 'A.F.' which appeared in the Sydney *Bulletin:*

Five fearful days beneath the scorching glare,
  Her babe she nursed,
God knows the pangs that woman had to bear,
  Whose last sad entry showed a mother's care,
'Then — nearly dead with thirst'

N

MEMORIAM

Mʀꜱ WATSON

THE HEROINE OF LIZARD ISLAND

COOKTOWN

NORTH QUEENSLAND

A.D. 1881

ERECTED 1886

EDWARD D'ARC

Mayor.

188